Building
Garden Ponds

Building Garden Ponds

Bryan Hirst

Voyageur Press

Printed in Malaysia

04 05 06 07 08 5 4 3 2 1

Library of Congress Cataloging-in-Publication Data available

ISBN 0-89658-042-3

Distributed in Canada by Raincoast Books, 9050 Shaughnessy Street, Vancouver, B.C. V6P 6E5

Published by Voyageur Press, Inc.
123 North Second Street, P.O. Box 338, Stillwater, MN 55082 U.S.A.
651-430-2210, fax 651-430-2211
books@voyageurpress.com
www.voyageurpress.com

First published in the United Kingdom by New Holland Publishers (UK) Ltd

Educators, fundraisers, premium and gift buyers, publicists, and marketing managers: Looking for creative products and new sales ideas? Voyageur Press books are available at special discounts when purchased in quantities, and special editions can be created to your specifications. For details contact the marketing department at 800-888-9653.

Editorial Direction: Rosemary Wilkinson
Project Editor: Clare Sayer
Production: Hazel Kirkman
Designed and created for New Holland by AG&G BOOKS
Project design (p 37, 53, 71 and 83): AG&G Books and Bryan Hirst
Photography: John Freeman, AG&G Books and Ian Parsons
Illustrator: Gill Bridgewater   Designer: Glyn Bridgewater

Conversion chart

To convert metric measurements to imperial measurements, simply multiply the figure given in the text by the relevant number shown in the table alongside. Bear in mind that conversions will not necessarily work out exactly, and you will need to round the figure up or down slightly. (Do not use a combination of metric and imperial measurements – for accuracy, keep to one system.)

To convert	Multiply by
millimeters to inches	0.0394
meters to feet	3.28
meters to yards	1.093
sq. millimeters to sq. inches	0.00155
sq. meters to sq. feet	10.76
sq. meters to sq. yards	1.195
cu. meters to cu. feet	35.31
cu. meters to cu. yards	1.308
grams to pounds	0.0022
kilograms to pounds	2.2046
liters to gallons	0.22

Contents

Natural pond
36

Planted stream
42

Kidney-shaped
pond
46

Circular pond
52

Formal canal
58

Pond with bridge
and beach
64

Raised pond
70

Pond with decking
76

Mosaic pond
82

Split-level pool
88

Introduction

O ver the last ten years I have spent much of my time studying, building and improving ponds and water features. The knowledge that I have gained will, I hope, give you the confidence to build your own uniquely beautiful water feature which will give you and generations to come endless pleasure and delight.

Because of modern technology it is now relatively easy and inexpensive to build a pond in your garden. This book outlines the principles and practices of building, planting and maintaining ponds which use flexible liners and modern materials, or traditional methods where appropriate, and is full of useful information.

This beautiful pond is the focal point in a classic garden. It requires careful planning and construction but is worth the effort (see page 58).

Once you have grasped the principles, there is no limit to what your location, imagination and hard work can achieve when it comes to building a pond in your garden. There are ten very different ponds in this book, ranging from informal, natural ponds to raised brick ones.

The music of falling water adds to the serenity and beauty of a garden pond. Many designs have room for a fountain or small water feature.

Water has a special significance in our lives. Apart from the fact that our bodies and souls need it to function properly, it has a calming and soothing influence. A pond at the heart of the garden is a captivating element – water and light can enchant the eye and lift the spirit. The achievement of true contentment is difficult at best and impossible without water. The importance of water, for me, was exemplified in the garden during an Indian summer evening. My daughter was mesmerized by the water skaters dancing between the lilies on the surface of the water, my partner was drinking a glass of wine listening to the waterfall, I saw the plants and the sky reflected on the water and looking deeper saw the fronds of the submerged plants teeming with life. All was well in the world that I shared and had helped to create. Perhaps the same delights await you.

Bryan R. Kirk.

Health and safety

If you are thoughtful and take care when working, any potential hazards are easily avoided. Before starting work, consider the following:

- ✔ Is it safe to build a pond in your garden if you have young children? (See page 13?)
- ✔ For some pond building procedures you will need to wear gloves, goggles and a dust mask and take some basic precautions. (See pages 20 and 22.)
- ✔ Make sure that you are strong and fit enough for the task ahead.
- ✔ Immobilize any equipment or lock it up and make sure that a safety barrier or tape stops anyone wandering unprepared into your excavation.
- ✔ Have a first-aid kit and telephone within easy reach. If possible, avoid working alone.

Part 1

Techniques

Designing and planning

Building a water feature is a big undertaking that involves a fair amount of hard work and as it is designed to be a permanent feature of the garden, planning is essential. The decisions to be made are based partly on what sort of pond you want, and partly on the limitations of your garden. These and the following pages suggest pond types, locations and functions to help you choose what suits your needs best.

Types of pond

Natural pond

This pond follows the forms and curves of nature, with no built-up edges, and perhaps includes an outcrop of stone or a beach. This allows for planting, where appropriate, in and at the edges of the pond and gives the impression that the water was there long before the rest of the garden and house were constructed.

Bog garden

Wet areas, often located next to ponds, support a wide range of plants that do not grow in ordinary garden conditions. Bog gardens can be built to stand alone or as part of an informal pond.

Above: For a natural-looking pond to be completely successful, the lining must be entirely hidden from view, especially at the edges. Restrained planting suitable for a natural pond is also a key feature.
Right: Include a boggy area in your pond design if you want to grow plants like this Arum lily, one of a large range of plants that will thrive with roots under water.

Above: As well as offering the delights of water lilies which will flower all summer long, this sunken formal brick pond brings the sky down to earth with constantly changing reflections and leads the eye down the full length of the pond.

Formal pond

A geometric design works best if it forms an association in materials and design with the buildings that are close to it. It may, for example, be rectangular, octagonal or linear in form, and may have a stone or paved edge that allows easy access to the water's edge. Where possible, any change of level can be exploited with small waterfalls running from the higher to the lower pond. Planting is possible in a formal pond, although this is more likely to be a few carefully chosen architectural plants, rather than a large number.

Raised pond

This is a formal pond constructed above ground level and contained by brick or stone walls. Its advantage is that it reduces the amount of soil that needs to be removed from the site; however, this saving is usually absorbed by the increased cost of construction of the exterior walls. As they will be a major feature, they often require finishing materials that can be more expensive than hidden construction materials, where the finish is not important.

Above: If a raised pond is at a comfortable sitting height (22 in. is ideal), it is fascinating to dabble or to watch the varied life in the pond life close up whilst enjoying a drink or contemplating life.

Stream or channel

The principles of creating a stream or channel are much the same. A stream is designed to appear entirely natural, whereas a channel is a formally contained stream. You can use a slope by creating an apparently natural source of water: this is achieved by pumping water to a disguised source, giving the impression of water coming up from a spring. The character of the stream or channel will be altered by the gradient of the ground. The steeper the gradient, the greater the potential for pools and waterfalls.

This gentle stream with planting along the edges allows you to make the most of a slight gradient. If your garden is steep enough, you can have waterfalls as the water makes its way down. The stream must nestle comfortably in the ground for it to look natural.

Locations

Marking the shape

When you have worked out all the possible locations for your pond, mark them out with lengths of rope or a garden hose, or even spray paint. Marking out the pond shape and viewing it from all aspects allows you to be sure that the end shape (which is difficult and expensive to change) is exactly what you expected. If you have the technology, it is worth photographing the area with a digital camera and manipulating the image to see how this can affect reality. Should any trees be reshaped, reduced or removed? Are there any natural dips or gullies that could be made to hold water, or any slopes from which water could run from fountain to pond? Is there a vista that you can reflect in the surface of your pond?

Above: The natural lie of the land will dictate the shape and character of a pond. Gentle curves are easier on the eye than sharp bends in informal settings. Nature abhors straight lines and perfect circles. Above right: This natural looking pond makes the most of its beautiful setting, allowing the reflections of the sky to reach up to the edge of the pond and tempting you down to the water's edge. The grassy bank edging the pond is perfect for sitting by the water on summer days.

Natural advantages

The surface of a pond reflects light and all the changing humours of the weather and seasons, and the placing of what is effectively a mirror surface to gain the most from this quality is something that should be given major consideration. Studying the movement of the sun across the horizon may give you an opportunity to create a dappled effect on the ceiling or walls inside your house, and to bring more light into a shady area. Place mirrors in the intended pond area to help evaluate the effect of the reflected light.

Visibility

To get the most from your pond it is often best to site it where you can see it from inside your house – perhaps from your bedroom window or the kitchen or recreation areas – so you can enjoy its appearance changing with the time of day as well as the seasons. Remember that the perceived shape of the pond will be altered by the viewpoint: for example, an oval pond will appear round when viewed along the greater length, as the apparent length will become reduced.

Alternatively, some of the most exciting ponds are sited away from a property and require a walk to them. If your garden is large enough, try to have some part of the pond not immediately visible from the house, as this encourages the adventure of a search and exploration of the grounds to reveal the whole picture.

Experiment with sound by adjusting the volume of water flowing over waterfalls and by positioning stones to alter the music.

Make sure that it is not possible to drive a car or other machinery into the water – for example, if the pond is to be near car parking areas or driveways, put up posts or raised curbs to physically stop any runaway machines.

Ease of use

Make sure that you can approach the pond easily and that there is going to be provision for seating near the pond on a flat surface. Consider placing a pergola, barbecue or dining area near the pond.

Stepping stones sunk into a lawn will allow you to approach the pond during the winter or when the grass is wet. Make sure that the stones are well set into the ground and will not interfere with the mowing. People naturally congregate by a pond so make enough space by it.

By-products

If your pond is to be dug out, rather than raised, consider what are you going to do with the excavated material. Can you build up a bank, or should you take the soil away, which can be expensive and difficult? If you are removing good topsoil, look at possible uses elsewhere to add to the quality of the soil, or to level another section of your property. It is easy to underestimate the amount that you will have to take away – often it bulks up and becomes up to a third more in volume than when it was in the ground.

Neighbors

If your project can be seen or heard by the neighbors, check that they have no objection to your proposed scheme. A rock waterfall, for example, will be heard by your neighbours and may cause them irritation. Excavations can affect the foundations of a neighbor's house or outhouses, fences or trees, as well as the water table or water supply to adjoining properties. If you consider that any of these factors could be a problem, consult an engineer.

Child safety

Children can and sometimes do get into trouble in ponds, and it is important to consider all potential hazards. A raised pond deters children from crawling or stumbling into it, or borders can be built around the inside perimeter of the pond to keep children out of water that is more than 3 in. deep. A custom-made decorative steel grid could be used.

The design of some fountains allows stones to be placed in the basin to reduce the depth of the water; these can be removed later when children have reached a safer age. Another alternative is to delay the project until your children have reached an age when they do not need constant supervision near water.

Sound

For many, the sound of running water from a stream or fountain gives an enormous sense of calm and relaxation. This sound may be tuned or adjusted by altering the volume of water that is flowing, or by placing obstacles, such as stones or rocks, in the path of the water.

Obstacles checklist

- ✔ Are there underground services, which may be affected by your workings? Check with the relevant utilities companies.

- ✔ Consider the type of soil and what lies underneath it: for example, solid rock will be expensive to break up and remove, clay soil requires hard work to dig deeply and it is impossible to make clean-sided holes in sandy soil.

- ✔ Could there be the foundations of an earlier building or construction?

- ✔ Are there any large plants or trees nearby which are likely to have wide spreading roots that you need to avoid cutting through?

- ✔ Has the ground been disturbed and polluted or made unstable?

Functions

The next consideration is what you want the water feature to do for you, and how important each of your requirements is, compared to each other.

Reflections

Watching still waters reflect the changing weather patterns in the sky can be immensely enjoyable, and these reflections are radically altered if water from a fountain falls on to the surface of the pond. A waterfall will ripple the surface and break up light reflections.

Falling water is fascinating; it catches the sunlight as well as causing ripples and breaking up the surface of the pool below.

As a natural pond matures, the surface of the water will be covered with plants. Arrange in groups or stands of the same plants together as the effect is generally more pleasing and the area is easier to maintain. Below: Wildlife will come naturally to your pond. Attempts to import wildlife are unsuccessful as each habitat will support particular life.

Entertainment

Waterside entertainment has some added magical properties: decking allows you to be over the water whilst eating or relaxing; lights placed near the pond reflect in the water to add to the waterside effect; and a barbecue and dining area close to the pond could be considered.

Activity

The scale of your pond may allow boating, fishing, diving and swimming, while even sitting on the edge with your feet in the water on a hot day can give real pleasure. Children may be able to play with model boats. In the evening, floating paper boats with candles in them on the water adds charm and a sense of calm.

Plants

The quality and range of plants that can be grown in and beside the pond affect its visual characteristics enormously. Plants can be positioned in or beside the pond, either in the ground or in suitable containers.

Wildlife

This should come naturally to a pond, although it is possible to encourage certain types of wildlife, such

as frogs and newts, by building a beach to allow ease of access. The size and depth of a pond will dictate the range and quantity of the wildlife that use it.

Fish

When a pond has had a year to develop, it can support a small number of fish without upsetting the delicate ecological balance. If, however, you want to keep a considerable number of ornamental fish, you will need to fit filtration and cleaning facilities. These vary in size and type, but be aware that some filtration units can take up an area of up to half the surface area of the pond. Power supplies are required and special pipework needs to be built into the pond; protection for plants must also be installed.

Birds

Ornamental ducks can become tame, and wild birds will often attempt to colonize a pond. If ornamental ducks are planned for your pond, you should build a floating island house where they can be safe from foxes and other vermin; a pebble beach should also be built where they will be encouraged to enter and leave the water, and set up an area where they can rest and be fed. This will also minimize and contain the damage that ducks can do to the surrounding flora.

Filtration should be considered to remove the added nutrients that birds add to the pond through their droppings. These nutrients encourage algae and weeds such as duckweed which can quickly make a pond unsightly.

These houses protect birds from vermin such as foxes. They are ideally placed on an island which saves you the daily task of penning and releasing your birds, as most vermin will not swim to attack ducks.

Birds can have a devastating effect on a newly established pond, as they damage young plants. If they are unwelcome, early discouragement before they start nesting should generally be effective. Herons also pose a threat to fish keepers as they will often come at first light and take fish from a pond. There are various ways to discourage them which may be used with varying success. Decoys are available as wrought iron structures that resemble herons but they are often ineffective as the real herons will notice the lack of movement and disregard them after some time. Netting is effective, if unsightly but there are some attractive metal grille options available. Herons like shallow water so a depth of water at the sides of the pond will also deter them.

Practicalities

With the basic design and planning in hand, the next move is to consider the wider effects of adding a pond to your garden – whether it would affect nearby property, for example. Consider your neighbors, talk over your plans and agree on the scheme before you start work.

Costs

Undertaking a project yourself is unquestionably the most cost-effective method, as long as you have researched and designed your project well, as most of the cost of building a pond is taken up by moving materials. Costs are hugely affected by access and the difficulties of materials handling, and by hidden factors, which may only be revealed during the excavation. Labor costs can be difficult to estimate, but materials, plant hire and fuel can be more easily estimated and priced. The more you know and are able to do yourself, the lower your costs. Check your bank account before starting, as there is nothing more depressing and morale-lowering than a half-complete project awaiting funds and energy.

Disruption

Unlike interior projects, the weather and amount of rainfall during a pond project can cause problems and increase the time taken to complete it. You know the weather in your area best – however, I do not recommend the undertaking of a project if you are likely to experience frozen ground conditions, heavy rain or intense heat during the work.

Careful routing and storage of building materials minimizes disruption to your household during the works. Earth, concrete and general debris have an uncanny ability to spread themselves over the house, car, driveway, clothes and machinery, and neighbors may complain if machinery is used or work is undertaken during unsociable hours.

Removal of excess materials

A skip container or storage site, easily accessible from the road, may be required. Make sure that the relevant authorities have been informed of your plans and have given any necessary approval. Because trucks may need to

unload materials, make sure that an out-of-the-way location is clearly signposted.

Works access

This may require the co-operation of neighbors and the removal of plants or fence panels, so plan carefully. The narrowest comfortable width for a wheelbarrow to pass through is 3 ft.; avoid sharp turns where possible, and prepare steps with wooden planks to enable loaded barrows to pass easily over them.

If you are thinking of using an excavator (see page 22), check the minimum width and height required. Note that an excavator needs additional turning space at the sides and it may damage the surface on which it turns, so protect any vulnerable surfaces with boards.

Supply of services

During construction you will need water and electricity. If the project is large, arrange a temporary supply to the key locations using extension cable and hose pipes, so that these services are not affected during the workings.

Pond liners

Until the modern development of manufactured flexible liners, ponds were lined in traditional ways and it is worth considering the possible advantages of using such materials for both aesthetic and practical reasons before making a choice for your project. Availability of materials and costs for additional work in using them can be offset against savings made in the purchase of a modern liner.

Non-flexible liners

Clay

For many years clay was the lining material used for ponds, lakes and waterways; the canals of Great Britain, for example, were mostly made waterproof with puddled clay. In some instances it is still the most cost-effective and best way to line ponds, especially where it is present in the subsoil and there is a plentiful water supply. That said, it has its limitations, as all clay ponds leak to a greater or lesser extent. This may be caused by plants, which put their roots through the clay lining, leaving fissures when the organic materials in the roots rot. It may be also caused by drought: if the water level drops the clay cracks, and when the level rises again water escapes through the cracks and erodes into channels.

Another possibility is that the clay has been mixed with some other unsuitable material that allows water to leach out. To minimize this, clay should be carefully compacted in layers. This is generally done with the tracks of excavators while the clay is still damp. In addition, it is difficult to raise the water level of a clay pond above its natural level, dictated by the surrounding land and water table.

Lead

This material is rarely used in practical ponds today, and water from a lead-lined container should not be drunk. It is, however, supremely long-lasting, as demonstrated by the Roman baths at

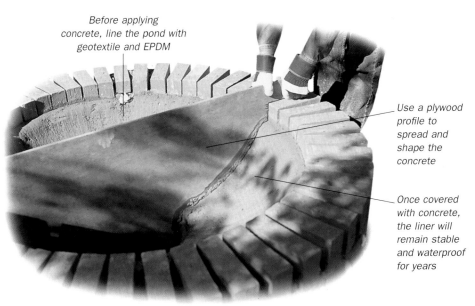

Concrete makes the ideal surface for covering with tiles or a mosaic. Before the concrete is applied, the pond should be lined with layers of geotextile and EPDM (see opposite).

Before applying concrete, line the pond with geotextile and EPDM

Use a plywood profile to spread and shape the concrete

Once covered with concrete, the liner will remain stable and waterproof for years

Bath, England which were made with a ³/4-in. layer of lead, dressed with stone – there is no record of this ever leaking. Lead is now available in rolls for roof work and can be used, when appropriate, to cover vulnerable or unattractive materials at the water's edge. After a few years it takes on a stable, mellow and attractive finish.

Steel

This is little used, but may have appeal if you are near a shipbuilding center, where it is readily available. It can be used to create attractive curves and natural shapes, and if good-quality steel is used and the pond is kept full of water, it should have an extended life.

Concrete

Until the arrival of EPDM and other flexible membranes, concrete was the favored material for the building of most garden ponds. It is rarely used today, as it is expensive and has a tendency to crack after some years and leak. When using concrete, it is important to reinforce it with a skeleton of steel and to ensure that the concrete is well prepared and vibrated to make sure that no air gaps are left in the fabric. Specialist contractors undertake this type of work. It is possible to repair concrete ponds under some circumstances, but the repairs are often unsatisfactory and difficult to make permanent.

Fiberglass

Using the same technology as that employed to make boats and certain car bodies, fiberglass can be an attractive option for small ponds where the shape and size are difficult to construct using a flexible liner. The material can also be dyed to any colour required. It is important that sufficient layers of fiberglass are laid down, and that the final gel coat is waterproof. Using fiberglass is an expensive option and is best undertaken by a specialist firm or experienced craftsman.

When fitting a premolded liner make sure that the voids underneath are carefully filled with sand. Back-fill around the pond, checking the levels as you go.

Preformed pond liners

These come in different shapes and qualities and are best used in very small-scale ponds where a particular shape is ideal for your purpose. When these are used it is important that there are absolutely no voids left between the liner and the sand in which it is buried, as these voids lead to stresses which can make the liner crack and leak. Large, irregularly shaped units with different depth zones must be supported properly or they may fracture.

Flexible liners

EPDM rubber liners

Flexible liners have made a huge difference to pond construction. One of the first flexible liners and still the best is EPDM rubber, which is used for a wide range of applications, from car windscreen sealant to tires, each made to a different formulation, principally using petroleum products. EPDM for pond liners is rather like the inner tubes of bicycle tires in appearance and characteristics, and while it is extremely flexible and stretches without breaking, it is very vulnerable to piercing with sharp objects (again like bicycle tyres). EPDM, therefore, needs to be protected from objects such as flints, sharp stones or gardener's forks. It can, however, be repaired if punctured by cleaning carefully and fitting with a rubber patch. Although it has a very long life, it can be damaged if exposed to ultraviolet light and should be protected with geotextile at all times, especially during construction.

PVC and other flexible liners

These liners are slightly cheaper than EPDM, but they share its vulnerability and have none of the benefits of flexibility and reparability. They tend to become brittle in a very few years, and rarely give a satisfactory long-term lining.

Geotextiles

These blanket-like materials – which are not waterproof – are used to stop flexible liners being penetrated by sharp stones and the like. Old carpet or padding, if non-organic and non-rotting, can be used for the same purpose when savings have to be made. Geotextile is available in various strengths, which are indicated by the weight of material per square metre. Generally, the greater the weight, the stronger and safer the product.

Do not walk on the liner unless you remove your shoes

Put just enough water in to hold the liner stable

Pull the liner up the sides and arrange any folds neatly

After you have positioned the EPDM liner, pour some water into the bottom as this will help in neatly arranging any folds or tucks. Adjust any folds as necessary as the water level rises. The pond can be left for a day or two to allow for further settling.

Lay the padding smoothly. Duct tape can be used to join the underlay and hold it in position while the liner is fitted.

Pumps, pipework and lighting

Pumps are used for fountains, streams and waterfalls and may be powered by solar- or mains-generated electricity. Part of the challenge when designing and building a pond is working out how to conceal and protect the electricity supply and water delivery pipes. Remember that water and electricity are a lethal combination. If you are in any doubt about fitting a pump or light, consult a professional.

Submersible electric pumps

These are ideal for most garden pond applications. Silent and invisible when placed at the bottom of a pond or in a balancing chamber, they comprise a sealed electric motor, generally run at mains voltages, and an impeller in a single casing. There are a large number available on the market, of all sizes.

Factors to be considered in choosing submersible pumps are:

- The length of the guarantee, now often three years or more.
- The effectiveness of the anti-clogging filtration system supplied. Generally, the larger the surface from which the water for the pump is drawn, the less quickly it will become clogged up.
- The volume of water pumped and the height to which it can be supplied. Check with your dealer when you have made the calculations.
- If the flow of water from a pump is too restricted it can heat up and damage the coils. Make sure that there is a bypass system fitted which allows the pressurized water to flow back into the pond. These are supplied with most pond pumps.

Non-submersible electric pumps

These are mainly used in industrial situations where large quantities of water are to be moved long distances. Easily maintained, they have the disadvantage of being noisy and require soundproofed housings which are liable to flood if placed below ground level.

Ram pumps

Where there is a natural flow of water near your pond, you may consider the use of ram pumps, which were widely used in the 19th and early 20th centuries. Using the force of a downward running stream, they force a small quantity of water up an incline. Still occasionally used today, they have the disadvantage of making a sharp tapping noise, and are best used where electricity or solar power are not available to run a modern pump.

Pipework

Where conduits are required for filters or a balancing chamber, good quality pre-formed pipework should be used – the pipework used for drainage in domestic situations is inexpensive and readily available. Use the largest practical bore for the pipework, as it is less likely to block up and create problems for maintenance. Always test the joints and couplings as, when the pond is filled, the joints will be under considerable strain, (more than in a drainage situation), caused by the head of water attempting to expand and burst the joints.

For land drainage or allowing water to drain away, use flexible plastic pipes perforated with many small holes. These pipes should ideally be buried in gravel, which will allow water to percolate through and run off (see page 26).

Lighting

A large number of lights are available for both exterior and underwater use. These are generally low voltage and have a transformer. All cables should be carefully hidden and protected from damage by gardening implements such as pronged forks. Underwater lamps should be placed so that the lenses do not become covered with detritus in the water, or if that is not possible, position them so that they can easily be cleaned. Water diffuses light, so place lenses close to the surface of the water.

Controls

Lighting and pumps can be controlled remotely from the pond, ideally from a situation where you can see the pond. However it is important to protect the controls from the weather. In planning electrical controls, it is wise to consult an electrician at an early stage. Modern contact breakers and RCD units should be fitted to any external electrical units, and any power supplies should be conducted in armoured cables capable of handling the required amperage without difficulty. All external fittings should be of a waterproof or weatherproof approved standard.

Water supply

This is usually taken from the house supply or a natural source such as a spring or stream. When an automatic topping-up system such as a ballcock is to be used, fit a non-return valve into the system in order to make it completely impossible for water to flow back from the pond into the mains supply (see page 27).

Pumps, pipes and lights

There is a large range of pumps available; generally the more you pay the better the quality. Your retailer will advise and ask two key questions: what amount of water is required and what height is it to be raised. Measure the height from the water surface to the outlet and explain the type of display you wish to achieve. Some outdoor light fittings can be used either around the edge of the pond, or as underwater lights.

Fountainhead
Some are adjustable like the nozzle on a garden hosepipe

Telescopic outlet pipe
Extends telescopically to suit different depths

Pipe reducer
For fitting different size fountain heads

Push-fit connector
Check that this is suitable for your set-up

Screw-fit connector
Ensures secure joints

T-junction
Facility for a tap and a second outlet pipe

Integral adjuster
Rotates to restrict flow

Pump and filter housing

Submersible pump

Power selector

Fixing plate

Reinforced garden hose

Flexible armored pipe

Flexible clear plastic pipe

Domestic drainage pipe

Perforated land drainage pipe

Joint for domestic drainage pipe
(various angles available)

Order a spare bulb when you buy any lamps

Cable outlet

Take care not to damage the liner when fixing the light

Underwater light

The glass features a structured surface which breaks the light

A bracket allows the light to be turned up to 180°

A garden spike can easily be attached to the bracket

Exterior light

Construction materials

In general, the fewer the number and type of materials involved in the construction of a pond and surrounding area, the more pleasing it is to the eye. If any particular type of brick or stone is used near the pond, make sure that you will be able to obtain replacements at a later date, in case any of them are damaged. Where possible use local materials. Architectural salvage yards are always worth investigating.

Concrete and mortar

Concrete

Used to form solid foundations and footings, the strength of concrete is dictated by the ratio (by volume) of sand and stones (ballast) to cement powder. For most pond construction work a ratio of 4 parts ballast to 1 part cement is ideal, but if large areas are to be concreted, it is worth considering reinforcing the concrete with steel mesh. Most cement manufacturers will be happy to advise you.

The amount of water used in a concrete mix affects its handling properties: the more water used, the sloppier the concrete. Too much water will affect the strength of the cured concrete. For most practical pond work the concrete should stand rather like stiff mashed potatoes, and it should be used quickly after it has been mixed, before it stiffens up. There is a range of proprietary additives that affect its properties, but these are expensive and can affect the strength, and I would suggest avoiding them unless unusual circumstances prevail.

Concrete should not be mixed or used when frost or below-freezing temperatures are expected, as they make concrete crumble and become useless. If there is a possibility of frost once you've laid the concrete, protect it with sacking or insulating material which stop it from freezing. Equally, if high temperatures are anticipated, protect concrete from drying out too quickly, using plastic sheeting, damp hessian cloths or sacking.

Mortar

This is the sand-and-cement mixture that is used to bond bricks and blocks together. It can be made in a variety of types and strengths: for building brick walls a mixture of 3 parts builders' sand to 1 part cement is standard. This can be colored if required, using readily available colorants.

Caution
The cement powder used to make concrete and mortar is corrosive. Always wear a dust-mask, gloves and goggles. If you get cement on your skin wash it off immediately with plenty of water.

Other materials

Gravel

Gravel is used for under-liner drainage as it allows water to pass through, and can also be used for beaches, paths and level areas. It is available in many grades, from fine pea gravel to gravel the size of a small egg. It can be bought washed or unwashed – the latter is cheaper.

Soil

Clay loam for putting in ponds should ideally be sterilized to kill any weed seeds that may be in it. Aquatic nurseries can supply small amounts; use sterilized, screened topsoil for large amounts.

Wood

Wood can be used for bridges, decking and garden buildings – and even as a surround for a formal pond. It is generally classified as either hardwood or softwood. Hardwood is slow-grown wood from deciduous trees such as oak, elm or ash, while softwoods are usually from pine or other evergreen trees. Most softwoods should be treated in order to stop them from rotting – especially if they are to be in contact with water. Check with the manufacturer that the treatment will not affect the fish or wildlife and avoid anything that has loose knots or splits.

Each type of tree has its own characteristics for strength, ease of handling and cutting, and resistance to water. Freshly cut oak (known as green oak), for instance, is ideal for decking applications as it lasts in water for more than 25 years. It takes on a lovely silver-gray color, and is relatively inexpensive and easy to work. Avoid beech wood and most other hardwoods unless you have checked its resistance to rotting in water. Carpenters or your wood supplier will advise you.

Use stainless steel, brass or galvanized bolts and screws as others will corrode and damage the wood.

Walling materials

Generally walling which will be seen ("facing work") is more expensive than hidden materials. Often walls have a backing of inexpensive bricks or blocks with a facing of high-quality bricks or stonework. Natural materials should be used wherever possible. Stone generally ages better than pre-molded materials although these are often less expensive and easier to work with. If you are in doubt, a builder's supplier will advise you.

Concrete blocks are generally weatherproof; however, some bricks are not resistant to water and frost and will fail if used in pond or exterior construction.

Calculating quantities

✔ Allow 10% over the calculated quantities to allow for wastage.

✔ Talk to your supplier before quantifying: some materials are measured in face square feet, some by weight and some by number of units.

✔ Concrete and mortar quantities quoted in this book refer to volumes (parts) and weights, eg. 1 part cement and 4 parts sand. The weights are only a rough guide to ordering; always mix by volume.

Paving materials

A vast range is available at widely differing prices, with natural stone the most expensive. If purchasing natural stone to edge a pond, remember that, unlike in most other situations, the depth of the stone is important because the edges of the pavers will be seen, so consistency in depth should be specified.

Manufactured pavers, made to look like natural stone, are also available. The better ones age well and become indistinguishable from natural stone when lichens and other materials age them. Others lose their color quickly and can become an eyesore, so choose carefully.

Construction materials

General home stores, builders' supply stores and architectural salvage yards will have a wide range of bricks, stone, wood and fixings. Explain the purpose and use as some may be adversely affected by water. You will find variations in price so check with different manufacturers. Sometimes you can reduce costs by

Brick

Boulder

Natural stone paving

Gravel

Manufactured paving

Slate

Cobbles

Coach bolt, washer and nut

Galvanized steel nail

Coated screw

Softwood post, plank and other useful sections

Sleeper

Tools

Tools are one of the main keys to successful pond-building. Although the best tools are no substitute for enthusiasm and determination, carefully chosen, top-quality tools will ensure that each and every task is accomplished with minimum effort and maximum efficiency, in the shortest possible time. It is fine to begin by using your existing tools for the projects – buy new ones if and when the need arises.

Level

Because water levels are flat it is vital that the edge of a pond is also built flat. The easiest way to achieve this is to use a long spirit level (3–6 ft. long is suitable) which can also be used in conjunction with a straight beam of wood. For large ponds (16 ft. in diameter or more) a number of wooden pegs can be hit in the ground and levelled with each other. A surveyor's level will give improved accuracy.

Excavator

Depending on the scale of your project and the availability of access, you can rent a tracked excavating machine, with or without an operator. The size and type of mechanical digger required for a job is related to the amount of work to be done – generally a 360-degree tracked excavator, ranging in size from 1 to 32 tons, is suitable. Your rental shop will be able to make recommendations when you outline the size of the excavations and your needs for handling material. If you are hiring a dump truck, make sure it is not too small for the job; again, advice from the rental company will be helpful.

Try to plan the work so that you do not disturb more ground than is necessary, starting in one area and working your way out. Precision with levels is important, as replaced subsoil is not as structurally sound as the virgin ground. Keep others well outside the danger areas where you are working.

Where the ground is soft and the area less than 9 ft. in diameter, digging by hand is the best way to create a pond. For larger areas consider using an excavator.

Hand digging tools

Chose your tools with care – a well-chosen, quality tool is a worthwhile investment. A good spade is particularly important if you are excavating the pond manually. For very hard ground you will need a spade with a narrow cutting edge but if the soil is friable you may approach with a shovel. Most hardware stores carry a good range. Generally metal tools are less expensive and more durable than wood or plastic handled tools. Gently does it if you are not in the habit of digging. You will use muscles unused to work so half an hour is the maximum you should work on the first outing; build up carefully after that. A sturdy wheelbarrow is an essential tool that will make lifting and carrying easier. Make sure you get the right size of wheelbarrow for the job: one that can be handled easily when full but is still large enough to be useful.

Concrete mixers

Although small quantities of concrete can be mixed by hand, the work is much eased by using a powered concrete mixer. These are generally powered by electricity or a gas engine. If electricity is available close to the workings, an electric mixer should be your preferred option as they are quieter and cheaper to run. Make sure you have a circuit breaker plugged into the power socket to protect you from electric shock if an accident occurs.

It is important to wash out the mixer thoroughly after each load is used up as otherwise the mortar or concrete will set in the drum and reduce efficiency as well as incur a cleaning cost when the machine is returned to the rental shop.

Safety equipment

- ✔ Sturdy boots with steel toecaps, available at builder's supply, are necessary for all pond construction.

- ✔ Gloves are vital during work with concrete, as your skin may react if in contact with concrete or mortar.

- ✔ Goggles are required if you are operating any grinding equipment, as is ear protection if you have to hire noisy machines.

- ✔ If you are involving an excavator, wear a hard hat.

- ✔ Make sure you have the number of the local hospital handy, and keep a first-aid kit close to hand.

A basic tool kit

A good set of tools makes pond building easy and the right tool can save you a lot of time. For the projects in this book, you will need a bucket, a wheelbarrow and some of the tools shown below. All of these can be bought from a local general store, or rented. Some specialist tools, such as a pick or mattock for hard ground are not shown but rental shop staff can advise on what you might need. A wooden board will be helpful for placing mortar on for brick laying. Garbage bags and a broom will be necessary for tiding up.

Gloves

Large tape measure

Pegs and string

Scissors

Spirit level

Spade

Line set

Mortar trowel

Fork

Brick chisel

Pointing trowel

Shovel

Sledgehammer

Angle grinder

Bricklayer's hammer

Club hammer

Rake

Tape measure

Square

Carpenter's pencil

Saw

Caution
Power tools

Electricity, early-morning dew, buckets of water and wet hands are a potentially dangerous combination. When you use a power tool or an electric cement mixer, make sure that you use it in conjunction with an electricity circuit breaker and switch off the power when not in use.

Drill

Drill bit

Claw hammer

Adjustable wrench

Cordless drill

Basic techniques

Pond building can be good fun especially when you have a clear understanding of the basic techniques such as marking out, laying concrete and building brick walls, and when you can handle the tools and materials with confidence. If you have never made garden projects before, start with something small and simple. If you need encouragement why not plan a big pond and get some friends to help?

Dress right for the job

Old clothes are fine, as they will get dirty, however overalls are readily available and have many useful pockets. A sound pair of boots is essential; personally I favor boots which have a steel toecap and are easy to get on and off. Gloves should be worn if your hands are soft or you are dealing with materials like concrete, which can irritate the skin.

Take plenty of breaks

Stop for at least ten minutes every hour to assess your progress, have a pause and plan the next stage. Do your calculations and order materials when you are fresh and take photographs of each stage of the progress; you will be able to show them

Getting started

proudly in years to come. Take your time, and bring in help if some part of the job will over stretch you. If you come across obstacles like huge rocks consider keeping them as part of your design.

Measuring and marking

Use the carpenter's maxim "measure it twice and cut it once" and always make a note of your measurements.

Keep a good-quality carpenter's pencil handy for marking out on wood.

When ordering bricks, blocks, sand and concrete allow 10% for wastage.

Road marking paints of various colors are available from builders' suppliers and are ideal for marking out lines. Clear the nozzles after each use.

A taut string line will ensure accurate digging

Before proceeding be absolutely confident in your setting out. Do not hurry this stage as any mistake will be difficult and costly to rectify and require fruitless labour.

Foundations

The purpose of foundations is to provide a level and stable base on which to build. Foundations should generally be twice as wide as the wall that is to be built on them. The depth of the foundations varies but for most pond work 10 in. is deep enough; however if the base material is unstable, or liable to crack and heave such as clay, it is wise to err on the side of caution and dig down to 20 in. Fill the majority of the void with gravel and compact it by beating it down with a heavy hammer or by using a vibrating compaction machine before filling up to the required depth with concrete.

Foundations need to be level; pegs set at the same level can be used as a guide to spreading the concrete

This trench will be filled with a layer of gravel and topped off with concrete

Most ponds require foundations and these are either "footings" (a narrow strip of concrete) or a slab. If you don't build foundations the pond may quickly disintegrate.

Laying concrete

Always wear gloves as splashes can irritate and burn the skin. If you do get concrete on your skin wash it off with plenty of water immediately.

When you are moving the concrete from the mixer to the point of laying, do not overfill the wheelbarrow, as any slops will be unsightly, kill grass and be difficult to clean up afterwards. Also a heavy wheelbarrow full of liquid can be hard to control over uneven ground.

Start in one corner and work backwards, achieving the finished level with your float or tamping bar before moving on to the next section. In the same way as you would ice a cake, put an appropriate amount of concrete in the middle and then spread and manipulate the concrete making sure that you have sufficient before pushing it down to the final level. Work only in one direction at a time and do not leave any unfinished sections before moving on. Do not be rushed by the person delivering the concrete to you (if you are so lucky) and leave it in the wheelbarrow until you are ready to receive it.

When you have finished laying a section, immediately clean all your tools and put the unused concrete to good use. Never be tempted to bury it.

Use a piece of wood to "tamp" the concrete level

Make sure that you have prepared the area before you start pouring concrete. Building a level wooden frame called "formwork" is sometimes the easiest option.

Brickwork

The main thing is to build the wall upright, in the right place and with all the layers or courses of brick or block horizontal with staggered vertical joints.

The key to success is in the mixing of the mortar, which ideally should have the consistency of stiff mashed potatoes; if it is too dry the bricks will not readily bond to it. However, if it is too wet, the bricks will slide about. If possible watch a bricklayer at work and try to emulate his mortar. Be careful not to add too much water at the end of the mixing process; if the mix becomes too wet the only way to stiffen it up is to add more sand and cement, which can easily result in the over filling of the mixer.

Trial and error is the only way to learn, however once you have got it right it is easy to do the same thing again, a bit like riding a bicycle.

Use a string line to show where the bricks should be laid by wrapping the string around a brick, pulling the line over another and pulling the ends apart until the line is straight. Do a dry run without any mortar just touching (or kissing) the line with the bricks without moving the line.

Allow for a 1/2-in. bed of mortar below the bottom brick and carefully re-set the line so that the top edge of the brick will kiss the line.

Remove the bricks and lay down the mortar so that the entire bottom of the brick is on mortar. Place each brick on to the mortar and bed it down until it is in the correct position. Place some mortar on the ends of each brick before placing it so that you will have a 1/3-in. joint between each brick. If a brick is too low, lift it from the mortar bed, add fresh mortar and re-bed it.

Do not hurry the early process, it will rapidly become easier. Once laid a brick should not be touched again as that movement will break the seal between the brick and the mortar; if this happens the brick must be removed and the mortar and the brick replaced. So be careful not to knock any new brickwork. Do not begin laying the next brick until you are completely satisfied that the last one is correctly positioned.

When a row of bricks is complete, remove the excess mortar by slicing it off with the trowel.

The pattern of the brickwork is called the bond and it is this decorative arrangement of bricks that gives a wall its strength; it is important that the vertical joints do not occur near each other, as it weakens the wall and looks unsightly.

Tap each brick down until it is straight and level

Bricks and mortar are the ingredients for a classic raised pond. Position the bricks carfully, avoid smearing them with mortar, and do a nice job of finishing the joints.

Preparing the pond area for lining

Because rubber and other liners are damaged by sharp objects such as flints it is critical that during the building of a pond they are protected. Old carpet (of a synthetic, non-rotting type) can be used as an underlay, although modern geotextiles are readily available and easier to work with in a secure way (see page 17).

Consider the subsoil where the pond is to be. If it is naturally draining and is not affected by the local water table, no further action need be taken; however, if the subsoil may hold some water (such as clay or shale for example) or the natural water table may come up during the winter, you will need to create an escape for any water that might accumulate under the liner. Dig a trench 1 ft. wide by 1 ft. deep from the lowest point in the

excavation, following the contours of the excavation towards the (downhill) lowest side of the site. End the trench 3 ft. out-

side the excavated area. Place a 4-in. perforated land drain in the trench and fill with gravel.

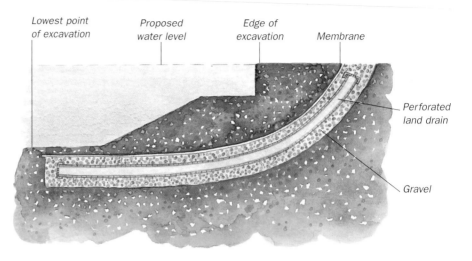

If the soil around the pond holds some water or if the natural water table rises in winter, a water escape trench will help deal with the water accumulating under the liner.

Pond lining

Positioning a flexible liner

With the liner roughly in place, take an edge in both hands and raise and lower it sharply. This produces a cushion of air between the liner and the geotextile and allows the liner to be drawn towards you. Repeat until the liner is correctly positioned, checking that the geotextile has

not been dislodged during the process. Stop further wind affecting the liner by weighing it down at the sides, taking care not to allow any sharp objects to come into contact with the liner. Fill the pond with enough water to hold the bottom securely, and tug at the edges to minimize any creases and folds (see page 17).

Fitting a non-flexible liner

The important thing is not to leave any voids beneath the liner, as when it is filled with water it will be strained and may crack. Try to dig the hole to match the shape of the shell, allowing for at least 1 in. of sand all round. When you have achieved this, shovel a small amount of sand all around the excavation. By placing and removing the shell you will be able to see all the places where the sand has touched the shell allowing you to build up the sand in areas where it has not touched. By repeating this procedure of adding and removing sand, the bottom section of the shell should sit evenly on a bed of sand. When you are satisfied that no more can be done by this method finally place the shell and fill up the voids at the side using a stick to push the sand and compact it. When the edges are nearly full put a hose into the sand and when the area is soaking compact the sand where you can to fill any remaining voids. It is then safe to fill the pond.

A line of bricks can be used to form a retaining edge to a planting shelf

Protective geotextile is used under the bricks and under the EPDM

Fill the pond with enough water to weigh down the EPDM

A flexible liner such as EPDM is suitable for any pond shape and should be laid on top of soft geotextile. Additional geotextile is used wherever there is risk of damaging the EPDM.

Repairing leaks in a flexible liner

Rubber liners can leak either because something is penetrating the liner or because it is undergoing stress brought about by stretching. In either case ensure that the cause is dealt with before undertaking the repair. The main difficulty lies in exposing the hole and making sure the surrounding area is clean and dry before you begin repairing the hole. A patch is made by attaching tape to a pre-sized piece of EPDM, leaving the waxed paper on the tape until the last possible moment. Although this is a fairly straightforward job it can be challenging on a muddy wet construction site, especially as cleanliness is essential to make permanent waterproof joints. Offer up the liners for joining making sure that the join will not be under strain when complete. Wash away any earth or materials that have stuck to the liner and clean an area at least 4 in. around where the join is to be made. Use gasoline to further clean the surfaces to be joined. Make sure the surfaces are dry with no rucks or pleats before taping together. Place the double-sided rubber tape between the cleaned surfaces. Using a heatlamp, warm the joined area by constantly moving the heat source so as not to burn the surface. When an area of about 1 ft. is warmed up turn off the heatlamp and wearing light gloves knead the join to ensure complete adhesion to both surfaces. Repeat the process on the next section of the join until the join is complete. Using scissors trim off any material left over next to the completed join. Carry out any repairs on a hot dry day.

Automatic top-up system

During dry summer months, the level of water in a pond may drop considerably. It can easily be topped up using a hose, however, on EPDM-lined ponds an automatic system can be built into the pond during construction. This uses the main water supply to keep the water level in the pond continually at the optimum level. This is particularly useful when the pond has fountains, streams or waterfalls which increase water evaporation.

Once you have excavated your pond, but before it has been lined, you will need to select the position for the automatic top-up chamber. This should be on rising ground ideally not more than 6 ft. from the edge of the pond. Buy a multibase drains inspection unit and enough 4-in. rigid pipe to reach from the chamber into the pond. These are available from most builders' supplies.

Excavate a hole large enough to contain the chamber and set it so that the top rim is at least 4 in. above the proposed water level in the pond. Stop up any unused pipe penetrations into the chamber. I use clear silicon around the clean stopper as an additional measure.

Dig a trench which leads from the chamber to the pond and attach the rigid pipe to the chamber so that it leads into the pond. Backfill around the chamber and pipe using soft sand.

When you come to line the pond you will need to cut a hole in the liner to allow the pipe to penetrate through without allowing water out. You can do this by buying a purpose-made penetration sleeve from the supplier of the liner. This can be attached to the liner using double-sided tape and heated to ensure a watertight joint. Bury flexible water pipe from the source of supply to the chamber. In colder climates this should be trenched in not less than 20 in. below ground to stop it from freezing during the winter. Connect the water supply to the main. When the pond is filled the water level in the chamber will be at the same level as the pond. Affix to the side of the pond an automatic flow valve adjusted so that the supply is turned off when the pond is full but turned on when the water level falls.

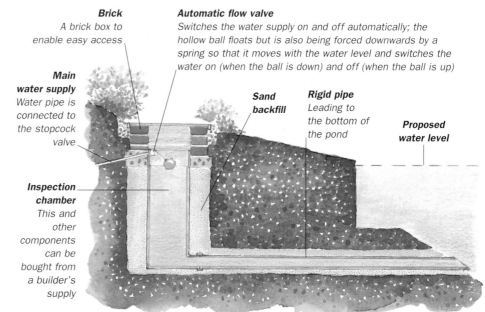

Brick
A brick box to enable easy access

Automatic flow valve
Switches the water supply on and off automatically; the hollow ball floats but is also being forced downwards by a spring so that it moves with the water level and switches the water on (when the ball is down) and off (when the ball is up)

Main water supply
Water pipe is connected to the stopcock valve

Sand backfill

Rigid pipe
Leading to the bottom of the pond

Proposed water level

Inspection chamber
This and other components can be bought from a builder's supply

An automatic top-up system like this one can be used for large ponds where there is a concern that the water level may drop rapidly in periods of hot dry weather.

Planting and development

The planting of a pond is, like the furnishing and decorating of a house, entirely a matter of personal taste. You may prefer an immediate complete scheme or to plant very simply and develop the project over a number of years, with each change or addition holding some personal significance or reflecting changing personal taste. The main thing is to find a knowledgeable plant supplier with a good range of stock.

Choosing plants

A mature pond with well established plants, rather in need of some routine maintenance and thinning. The ideal is to have one third of the surface of the water covered with plants as too much shaded area lowers the oxygen levels of the pond. Overcrowded plants are more prone to pests and diseases.

Plants can be moved easily, and the scheme can be altered as the various plants develop. Bold clumps with just a few classic plants generally have a more pleasing effect than a large number of different species. Simpler is generally better although your choice of plants will depend on the style of your pond.

Many aquatic plants are available by mail order. There are five categories:
- Submerged, also known as oxygenators or pondweeds
- Floating
- Floating-leaf
- Shallow-water or bog
- Marginal aquatic

Submerged plants (oxygenators or pondweeds)

These are the first plants that should be put into a newly completed pond for two reasons. First, they start putting oxygen into the water and grow rapidly during the growing season; and second, they generally have secondary forms of pond life in them, such as water fleas and daphnia which, as long as there is no competition, rapidly reproduce, creating a richer environment that encourages other forms of beneficial pond life.

It is worth visiting your local pond shop to see what oxygenators they have available, but take care that they are native to your environment, as some imported plants can grow rampantly and are unable to provide food or shelter for native forms of pond life.

Weigh down oxygenators with small metal collars (which can be obtained from aquatic supply shops) so that they take root at the bottom of the pond. Excessive amounts of pondweed should be thinned out during the summer months, by hand or using a plastic rake.

Floating plants

These obtain their nutrients from fine root hairs that they suspend in the water. It is important that floating plants are not allowed to cover too much of the surface of the pond, as they can stifle the submerged plants that depend on light filtering down through the water. If they become over-vigorous, they can be raked out. Some plants are liable to frost damage and should be brought indoors during periods of extreme cold.

Floating-leaf plants

One of the most popular floating-leaf plants are water lilies with round or oval leaves, which are suitable for any depth of water up to 68 in. deep. There is a wide range available with a variety of leaf sizes, and if you live in a tropical region, a more exotic range is available.

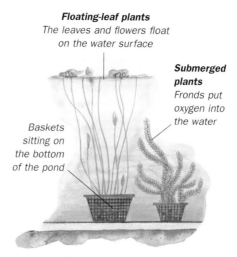

Floating-leaf plants
The leaves and flowers float on the water surface

Submerged plants
Fronds put oxygen into the water

Baskets sitting on the bottom of the pond

Submerged plants and floating-leaf plants both need to be rooted at the bottom of the pond (refer to plant labels).

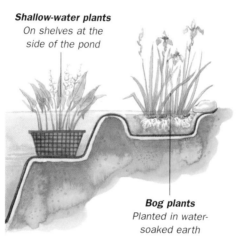

Shallow-water plants
On shelves at the side of the pond

Bog plants
Planted in water-soaked earth

Shallow-water and bog plants have very different needs – read the plant labels and ask for advice before purchasing them.

Marginal aquatic plants
These plants like continuously damp (but not wet) soil

Marginal aquatic plants require frequent watering until they are established. Choose larger species for a dramatic effect.

Floating-leaf plants should be grown in pots placed upright on the bottom of the pond at levels to suit. Remove excess and dying leaves, cutting the stems as low as practical in the water.

Lilies need to be thinned and divided after a number of years. Lift the plants in their baskets to the side of the pond and, using pruning shears, cut the corms into two sections, making sure that both halves have roots, flower heads and leaves. Cut back long or damaged roots and replant in clay or aquatic soil in perforated pots with the corm just showing above the soil, and cover with gravel to hold the earth in place.

Shallow-water and bog plants

Planted on planting shelves, bog areas or in containers at the edge of a pond, perennial shallow-water plants grow up quickly in the spring and die down in the autumn. Some forms of plants, such as rushes and grasses, which remain standing in the winter, will provide color and form during the winter months. They should be divided in the autumn after two or three years. Some plants require different care and conditions so read the labels carefully and plant accordingly.

Marginal aquatic plants

These may be much larger than the shallow-water and bog plants that grow at the water's edge. During the winter months they offer contrasting scale, color and form, and may produce reflections off the water. It must be remembered that, although they are next to the pond, they are outside the wet area and unable to take water from the pond so that they may require additional watering during the early years while they establish themselves and develop. Be aware that while some plants might be called marginal plants – like some species of bamboo – they are so fast growing that the sharp roots can damage a flexible pond lining. You should build a barrier or avoid them.

Maintenance

The hard work of building the pond may be over, but regular, simple maintenance is vital if it is both to look its best and attract the wildlife that develop a working ecosystem (see page 32). But what could be better on a bright spring day than to put on rubber boots and wade around in water and mud? Take this opportunity to inspect pumps and pipework, clean out clogged filters and make necessary repairs.

Pond maintenance

Every pond will need some kind of maintenance, although deep ponds tend to remain cleaner than shallow ones. Most of the jobs are quick and easy to do and are aimed at removing obvious debris like leaves and twigs, checking the balance of plant life which may entail raking away algae, weeding out over-dominant plants and reducing the number of fish. Occasionally you will need to change the water and repair any damaged liner (see page 27).

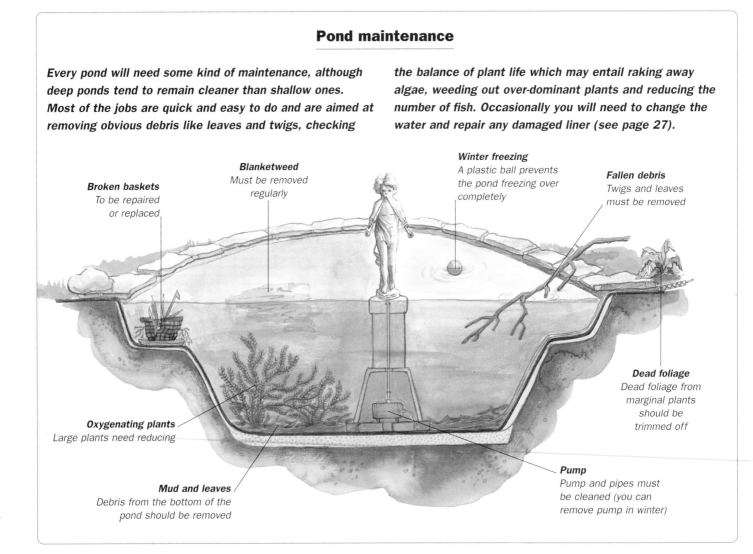

Broken baskets
To be repaired or replaced

Blanketweed
Must be removed regularly

Winter freezing
A plastic ball prevents the pond freezing over completely

Fallen debris
Twigs and leaves must be removed

Dead foliage
Dead foliage from marginal plants should be trimmed off

Pump
Pump and pipes must be cleaned (you can remove pump in winter)

Mud and leaves
Debris from the bottom of the pond should be removed

Oxygenating plants
Large plants need reducing

Routine maintenance

Controlling algae

Algae, particularly blanketweed, often proliferates on a garden pond, particularly when it is new and has not achieved a balanced ecosystem or is overstocked with fish. While there are a large number of preparations and suggestions for controlling algae, many of these have detrimental long-term effects. During the spring and early summer, remove algae on a frequent basis, using a plastic garden rake. As the growing season progresses and the pond's ecosystem develops, algae will grow with less vigour.

Plant maintenance

Controlling plants, so that one species does not dominate and inhibit other plants, can be done throughout the growing season as need dictates. In particular, floating-leaf plants should be watched carefully. Weeding unwanted species should be done little and often on a weekly basis, especially during the spring.

Fallen leaves floating on the pond surface sink in time and add to the detritus that accumulates at the bottom of a pond. In order to delay the time when a pond needs clearing out, these should be raked off and removed. For a small pond a net, spread over the pond's surface during the autumn, will facilitate this task.

Cut back and remove dead plant life during the autumn or, if you prefer, late in winter, just before the spring growing season. If the pond has a liner avoid using sharp-pronged metal tools and generally take care not to cause damage.

When to clean out

Because of the constant input of detritus into ponds, all need cleaning out from time to time, otherwise you will notice after some years that the characteristics of the pond become altered – the water becomes dark and cloudy, and the plants and wildlife that used to thrive start to die out. Cleaning work is generally best done in the spring or early summer, not least because the water is warmer and more pleasant to deal with.

Clearing and cleaning the pond

Start by pumping out the pond, using a submersible pump with a flexible hose, taking care to run the water into a drain or somewhere it can percolate away slowly without doing damage. Take care to preserve the fish or wildlife that you find as the water level drops, transferring the

Occasional maintenance

fish to a temporary container (a clean plastic dustbin is suitable), making sure that the water in it is well provided with oxygen, or the fish may suffocate. Putting an air pump into the holding container generally takes care of this problem.

Once the pump has taken out all the water that it can without becoming blocked, remove the rest of the detritus using a bucket and soft scoop. There is a real danger of damaging pond liners whilst they are unprotected by water, so make sure that no metal or sharp objects are used in this operation; also make sure that no sharp stones are trapped in the soles of boots. Do not be tempted to use any detergents or cleansing agents.

Remove the majority of the detritus – but not all. It is important to allow a certain amount to remain, as it contains enough of the microscopic pond life to

Care of fish

Remove and re-site fish if they have bred and their numbers and size are greater than originally planned. They are easiest to catch in the autumn, as the water temperature lowers and they become sluggish. If a pond is overstocked, fish become prey to disease and stresses. It is no kindness to the fish to allow them to breed and grow without control.

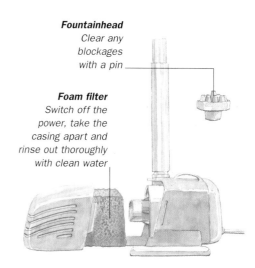

Fountainhead
Clear any blockages with a pin

Foam filter
Switch off the power, take the casing apart and rinse out thoroughly with clean water

Clean your pump regularly. If dirt and weed build up in the filter, the pump will fail.

recolonize the pond. Cleared detritus should be allowed to dry beside the pond and then be removed in sacks or placed on a compost heap, where it will rot down to provide an excellent compost.

Now is an excellent time to carefully assess the plants and divide any whose root systems are now accessible.

Any pumps and pipes should be carefully inspected and cleaned or replaced.

Restocking the pond

The pond can be refilled with water from a hose or, in ideal circumstances, with stored rainwater. Consider the number of fish that you have taken out of the pond and re-site some if necessary. Allow as long as possible before reintroducing fish into the pond to allow the water temperature to stabilize and give the ecosystem a chance to re-establish.

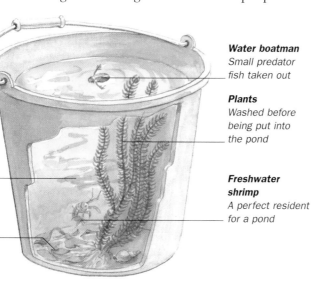

When you buy new plants use a quarantine bucket which allows you to select precisely what you do and don't want in your pond.

Blanketweed
Blanketweed must be removed

Decaying plants
All dead plant material pulled away

Water boatman
Small predator fish taken out

Plants
Washed before being put into the pond

Freshwater shrimp
A perfect resident for a pond

Balancing the ecosystem

Natural life will come quickly to your pond, and the ecosystem within it will start to develop as soon as it is filled. It is important not to disrupt this development by prematurely introducing fish or birds that short-circuit the ongoing development of the life of the pond. For a natural-looking pond you should choose plants and fish that are native to your area and avoid adding too many plants in the first instance.

Developing an ecosystem

The speed and development of the pond life are affected by three major factors relating to the water: nutrients, temperature and oxygen. These can be gradually manipulated through design, planting, stocking and maintenance to achieve the desired effect.

Nutrients in the water

These arrive in water, from the air, from rotting and dying plant material and from the excretions of fish and birds. If there are too many nutrients, the natural cycles which cope with the detritus break

This pond requires some basic maintenance (see page 30). The plants could be reduced, there is a lot of detritus that needs removing and surface weed that can be removed.

down, the water becomes entirely opaque and the system starts to smell unpleasant. In addition, nutrients in the water and high water temperature encourage the growth of algae, especially in the spring before pond plants have developed to absorb the excess nutrients.

Problems with algae are best avoided rather than cured. This can be done in a number of ways:

- Design the pond so that water that may have fertilizer dissolved in it does not run into it.
- Make the pond deep and large enough so that the water temperature does not rise too high.
- Plant shade-providing and nutrient-absorbing plants in and around the pond.
- Do not overstock with fish or birds.
- Provide consistent maintenance (see page 30).
- Inject oxygen into the water to aid the breaking down of nutrients.

Water temperature

This is to a great extent dictated by the weather and ambient temperature; however, the deeper the pond, the less immediately responsive it will be to day-to-day changes in the weather, and the more stable it will become. There is a natural cycle, rather like the weather, in which water circulates, bringing oxygen in the water to all parts, encouraging plants and wildlife, and helping with the breaking

down of nutrients. It is principally for this reason that it is worth digging a pond as deep as is practical. Although you may be tempted to reduce costs by saving in depth, in the long term this always leads to a reduction in stability and to increased maintenance costs. Something of the same effect of depth of water can be achieved by pumping oxygen into the water; however, as with all artificial environments, it can never be as desirable or stable as an environment that works simply with nature.

Oxygen in the water

As for us, oxygen provides life in a pond: it is absorbed by the water from air passing over it, water spilling through air, and by the photosynthesis of plants in the water. The more oxygen there is in pond water, the healthier it will be and the more life it will sustain. It also aids the decomposition of detritus in the pond, helping to keep the environment healthy and dynamic.

Oxygen can be injected into water to aid the breaking down of nutrients. This can be done either by using an air pump to pump air to the bottom of the pond, as we see with domestic fish tanks, or by throwing the water into the air, as with fountains and waterfalls.

Water filtration for fish

If a pond is designed for wildlife it will be able to sustain a small number of ornamental fish without upsetting the ecology and appearance of the pond. If however, fish are to be the predominant life in the pond, and there is no freshwater supply, you will need to install a filtration system. Filtration systems – often housed in a specially constructed unit adjacent to the pond – remove nutrients in suspension or solution in the water by passing the water over a series of filters before being returned to the pond. They are usually made up from a sponge or filter to remove sizeable solids from the water and a biological filter which works in the same way as a sewage plant by passing the water over a large surface area containing bacteria which absorb and convert nutrients into a non toxic form. In addition, an ultraviolet light kills bacteria growing in the water.

In addition to filtration, air may be pumped into the water to add to its oxygen content. If you fancy adding a dramatic feature to the pond then a waterfall, cascade or fountain also keeps the water oxygenated and fresh.

A beautiful example of a natural-looking pond. Clear water, thriving plants (maybe some of the plants could be reduced), the presence of fish, frogs, gnats, water snails and dragonflies, all suggest that the ecosystem of the pond is well balanced.

Part 2
Projects

Natural Pond

★
Easy

Perhaps the simplest and least expensive type of pond to create, a natural pond will fit in almost anywhere where there is a lawn or flat area in the garden. Carefully sited, it can offer stunning reflections, bringing the sky down to the earth as well as the delights of plant life both on and below the surface of the water. Once planted, wildlife will quickly come, be it frogs, newts, dragonflies or water beetles.

**Making time
3 weekends**
Three days for digging the hole and three days for lining and building the edges

Considering the design

If you have decided that this is the pond for you, consider the impact it will have on your garden. Ideally you need a completely flat, level surface but it can be positioned where there is a slight slope, as we did. As long as your foundation trench is level, it doesn't matter if part of your pond edge wall is above ground level; simply fill the area behind the wall. A good idea is to mark out the area of pond (as large as possible) and imagine what you would do in your garden with the pond in place. Only once you are convinced of the practicality and correct siting of the pond should you proceed. Consider what you are going to do with the spoil, how you are going to move it and by what route and tell the neighbors of your plans.

Getting started

Assemble your materials and equipment. Choose a dry day but make sure that you have somewhere to store your cement (off the ground and covered with waterproof material) should it suddenly rain while the work is in progress. Remember the final shape and depth of your pond will alter any quantities given.

You will need

Materials

- ✔ Concrete: 1 part cement (300 lb.) and 4 parts ballast (1,200 lb.)
- ✔ Sand: 2,200 lb. kg
- ✔ Geotextile: 46 sq metres
- ✔ EPDM: 1 piece 19½ ft. x 19½ ft.
- ✔ Bricks: 200
- ✔ Mortar: 1 part cement (50 lb.) and 3 parts sand (150 lb.)

Tools

- ✔ Tape measure, spray marker and pegs
- ✔ Wheelbarrow and bucket
- ✔ Spade, fork and shovel
- ✔ Club hammer
- ✔ Spirit level
- ✔ Pickaxe or mattock
- ✔ Rake
- ✔ Scissors
- ✔ Bricklayer's trowel

Overall dimensions and general notes

The design results in a completely natural-looking pond with no lining visible at the sides

The pond is approximately 13 ft. long and 10 ft. wide

Up to a third of the water's surface may be covered with plants once the pond has matured. Keep at least one aspect of the pond free for marginal planting.

Cross-section detail of the natural pond

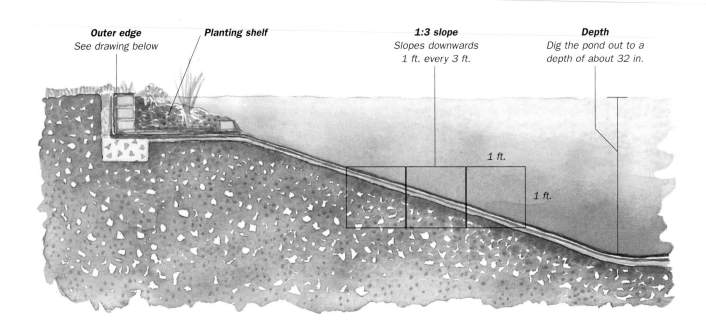

Outer edge
See drawing below

Planting shelf

1:3 slope
Slopes downwards
1 ft. every 3 ft.

Depth
Dig the pond out to a
depth of about 32 in.

1 ft.

1 ft.

Cut-away detail of the natural pond

Bricks
Three courses of
bricks around
the outer edge
of the pond

Planting shelf
Filled with earth to conceal
the bricks and geotextile

Marginal plant
Be careful when planting
not to damage pond lining

EPDM
Fold the EPDM over
the edge of the bricks
and trim off the excess

Bricks
A row of bricks
around the inside
edge of the planting
shelf holds the
geotextile in place

Geotextile
Trim the geotextile
level with the bricks

Sand
Half fill the cavity
with sand and top
off with earth

EPDM

Concrete foundation
1 ft. wide and
4 in. deep

Sand

Geotextile

Geotextile
An additional layer of
geotextile protects the EPDM
from getting damaged

Cut-away plan view of the natural pond

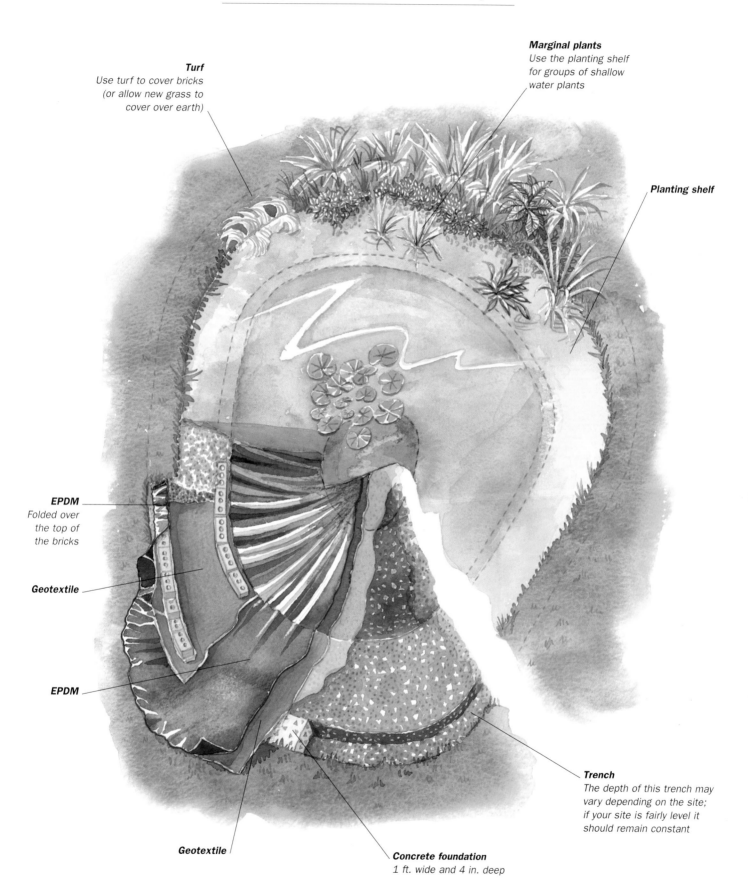

Turf
*Use turf to cover bricks
(or allow new grass to
cover over earth)*

Marginal plants
*Use the planting shelf
for groups of shallow
water plants*

Planting shelf

EPDM
*Folded over
the top of
the bricks*

Geotextile

EPDM

Geotextile

Concrete foundation
1 ft. wide and 4 in. deep

Trench
*The depth of this trench may
vary depending on the site;
if your site is fairly level it
should remain constant*

Making the natural pond

1 Digging the foundation trench
Use the tape measure and spray marker to set the shape of the pond out on a level area of ground. Use the spade to dig a narrow trench to a level depth of about 1 ft. all around the pond. If your site does slope ensure the trench is a minimum of 1 ft. deep.

2 Setting out a level footing
Check that the bottom of your trench is roughly level all around. Hammer in a series of wooden pegs approximately 32 in. apart so that they poke above the ground by 4 in. and the tops of the pegs are all exactly level with each other.

3 Filling the trench
Fill the trench with concrete up as far as the level of the top of the wooden pegs. The level brick wall will go on top of this concrete so make sure that you have spread the concrete evenly. A slightly sloping site may require building up with earth after the wall is built.

4 Excavating the pond
Using the pickaxe or mattock, spade and shovel, dig the pond out to a maximum depth of about 32 in. – complete with a planting shelf and a 1:3 slope (refer to the drawings on page 38).

5 Laying the geotextile
Remove all loose earth and sharp stones and cover the entire surface with a bed of raked sand. Cover the sand and the foundation with geotextile.

6 Laying the EPDM
Carefully spread the liner over the whole pond (see page 26 for useful tips), ensuring you have at least 1 ft. of liner overlapping the edge of the pond all around. Pour a small quantity of water into the pond to hold the liner in place.

7 Edging the planting shelf
Cover the planting shelf with scraps of geotextile. Lay a row of bricks (without mortar) around the inner edge of the planting shelf to hold the geotextile in place. Do not worry about these bricks being visible – they will soon get covered in mud.

8 Building the pond edge wall
Lay three courses of mortared bricks around the outer edge of the pond, checking the level with each course. Add a mixture of mud and waste mortar in blobs around the inner edge of the dry bricks.

9 Trimming the lining
Fold the geotextile and EPDM sandwich up and over the outer wall towards the middle of the pond. Fill the cavity between the wall and the surrounding earth with sand (do not use sharp tools). Trim the geotextile layers level with the top of the wall.

10 Finishing
Fill the planting shelf with earth, dig in your plants and top up with water. If the wall stands above the level of the ground, build up the area behind it with soil. Leave the EPDM overlapping the wall and cover the exposed edge of the pond with spare topsoil or turf.

Planted stream

Where there is sloping ground, a natural-looking planted stream is an option. This can lead down to a pond (one like the natural pond on page 36 is suitable) from which water can be pumped. It can meander with pools and eddies if the slope is a gentle one, or have waterfalls if the ground is steeper. The sound of the water can add to the delight of an environment that a wide range of interesting plants will thrive in.

★
Easy

Making time
3 weekends
4 days for digging and lining and a weekend to complete

Considering the design

The slope will affect the nature of your stream and the lie of the land; remember that water cannot run uphill! Study natural streams to see how a stream runs between obstacles and runs faster where the ground is steeper. If there are any natural clefts or gullies in your garden make use of them or move them to where you want your stream to be. Make sure the stream sits in, rather than on the surrounding landscape. Most problems arise when the stream is running and the water rises above the EPDM at the edges! You will need constant power and water supplies for this project. Remember that a toddler can drown in as little as ⅓ in. of water so even a shallow stream like this one can pose a potential danger. Never leave children unsupervised.

Getting started

Plan the route of your stream and establish that the starting point is higher than the finishing point, that the sides of the liner will be at least 4 in. higher than the finished water level (even when the stream is running) and that this is below the ground level around the stream. Where rocks are to be placed to form a pool and waterfall the water will rise up to 2 in. above the obstruction.

Overall dimensions and general notes

Stones constrict the flow of the water and make more splash

Fish are drawn towards the bubbling oxygen-rich water as it enters the pond

Run the stream into an existing pond or build a new one (see the natural pond on page 36) about 6 ft. in diameter or larger. The materials listed will make a stream about 32 ft. long and 2 ft. wide.

You will need

Materials
- Flexible armored pipe: 2 in. x 40 ft. long
- Geotextile liner: 43 sq yd.
- Duct tape
- EPDM: 1 piece 32 ft. x 6 ft.
- Concrete: 1 part cement (250 lb.) and 4 parts ballast (1,000 lb.)
- Mortar: 1 part cement (65 lb.) and 3 parts sand (280 lb.)
- Stones: 1 cu. yd.
- Land drainage pipe: 6½ ft. long
- Submersible pump
- Mastic

Tools
- Tape measure and spray marker
- Spade, fork and shovel
- Hacksaw
- Scissors
- Bricklayer's trowel

Cut-away view of the planted stream

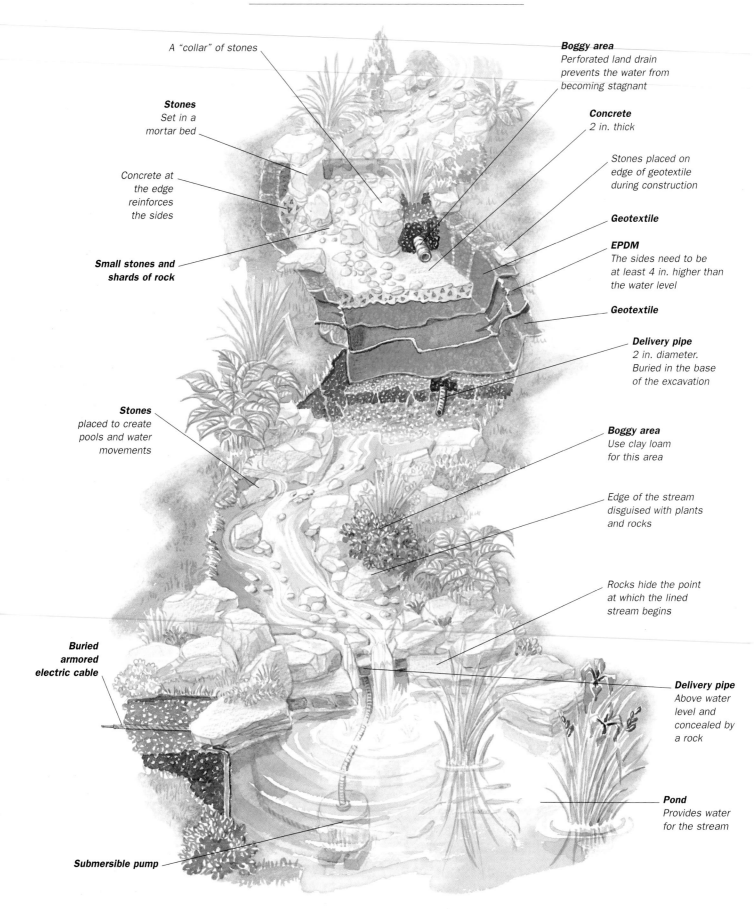

A "collar" of stones

Stones
Set in a
mortar bed

Concrete at
the edge
reinforces
the sides

**Small stones and
shards of rock**

Stones
placed to create
pools and water
movements

**Buried
armored
electric cable**

Submersible pump

Boggy area
Perforated land drain
prevents the water from
becoming stagnant

Concrete
2 in. thick

Stones placed on
edge of geotextile
during construction

Geotextile

EPDM
The sides need to be
at least 4 in. higher than
the water level

Geotextile

Delivery pipe
2 in. diameter.
Buried in the base
of the excavation

Boggy area
Use clay loam
for this area

Edge of the stream
disguised with plants
and rocks

Rocks hide the point
at which the lined
stream begins

Delivery pipe
Above water
level and
concealed by
a rock

Pond
Provides water
for the stream

Making the planted stream

1 Excavating
Dig out the entire area to a depth 4 in. below the projected stream bed. Put in the 2 in. flexible pipe which will deliver the water from the pump to the source, and bury it in the base of the excavation.

2 Laying the liner
Remove any sharp objects from the bed of the excavation, then cover with a layer of geotextile, securing any joins with duct tape. Line the stream area with EPDM, ensuring that at least 4 in. remains above the predicted water level where the stream will run.

3 Spreading the concrete base
Cover the lined area with another layer of geotextile followed by a 2-in. thick layer of concrete. Do not worry too much about creating a perfectly smooth finish as stones will cover most of the area. Leave to cure overnight.

4 Sculpting the watercourse
Lay down a mortar bed, shaping the watercourse as required and covering the stream bed with stones before the mortar has cured. A clay loam is ideal for the bog garden area. For a natural look, use one type of rock. In the boggy areas, perforated land drain should be placed in the deepest part to stop the water from becoming stagnant.

5 Installing the pump
Make sure the delivery pipe is above water level and disguise it with a one or more rocks. Attach a submersible pump and an adjustable valve to the lower end of the pipe and immerse it in the pond. Run the stream at the maximum possible ensuring there is no spillage over the sides of the EPDM.

6 Trimming and finishing
Cut away any excess geotextile and EPDM, covering the edge with earth or stones and hiding the point where the lined stream begins. Reduce the water flow to the desired pace and plant the bog areas. If you modify the stream at a later date check the liner sides again!

Kidney-shaped pond

Because the size and shape of this project are easily adjustable this pond can fit most gardens. The smart brick edging allows you to walk around the pond throughout the year without getting muddy or wet shoes and it could easily fit into a patio scheme or be surrounded by grass, gravel or a sweeping brick path. When you mark out the organic kidney shape try to avoid it getting too narrow at any point.

Making time
6 weekends
Three days for excavating the hole and the remaining time to complete

Overall dimensions and general notes

Make sure that the size of the pond does not interfere with access to the garden.

The depth of the water will be affected by the shape of the pond; do not make it too narrow at any point

17 ft. long

11½ ft. wide

Look for bricks that match the house so the pond blends in

You will need

Materials

- ✔ Geotextile: 65 sq yd.
- ✔ Duct tape
- ✔ Butyl sheet: 1 piece 25 ft. x 20 ft.
- ✔ Concrete: 1 part cement (400 lb.) and 4 parts ballast (1,200 lb.)
- ✔ Mortar: 1 part cement (90 lb.) and 3 parts sand (270 lb.)
- ✔ Bricks: 210 for the retaining walls and 120 for the coping
- ✔ Sand: 770 lb.

Tools

- ✔ Tape measure, 50 ft. long hose (for marking shape), spray marker and peg
- ✔ Spirit level
- ✔ Club hammer
- ✔ Spade, fork and shovel
- ✔ Scissors
- ✔ Bricklayer's trowel
- ✔ Pointing trowel

Considering the design

This pond can be shaped to suit the garden where a formal or geometric shaped pond is not required. The edges can be marked out with a garden hose, and viewed from all sides before the final shape is chosen. Remember that the further away from a round shape that the pond finally forms, the more difficult it will be to get an adequate depth of water. Deep water will, in the long term, reduce maintenance requirements and aid the pond's ecology, reducing blanketweed, for example. Never leave children unsupervised near a pond.

Getting started

Trim back or remove any existing plants that may be affected by the works. Consider what you are going to do with the excess soil, how you are going to move it and by what route and tell your neighbors about your plans. Assemble your materials and equipment. Choose a dry day but make sure that you have somewhere to store your cement (off the ground and covered with waterproof material) should it suddenly rain while the work is in progress. Remember the final shape and depth of your pond will alter the quantities given above.

Cut-away detail of the kidney-shaped pond

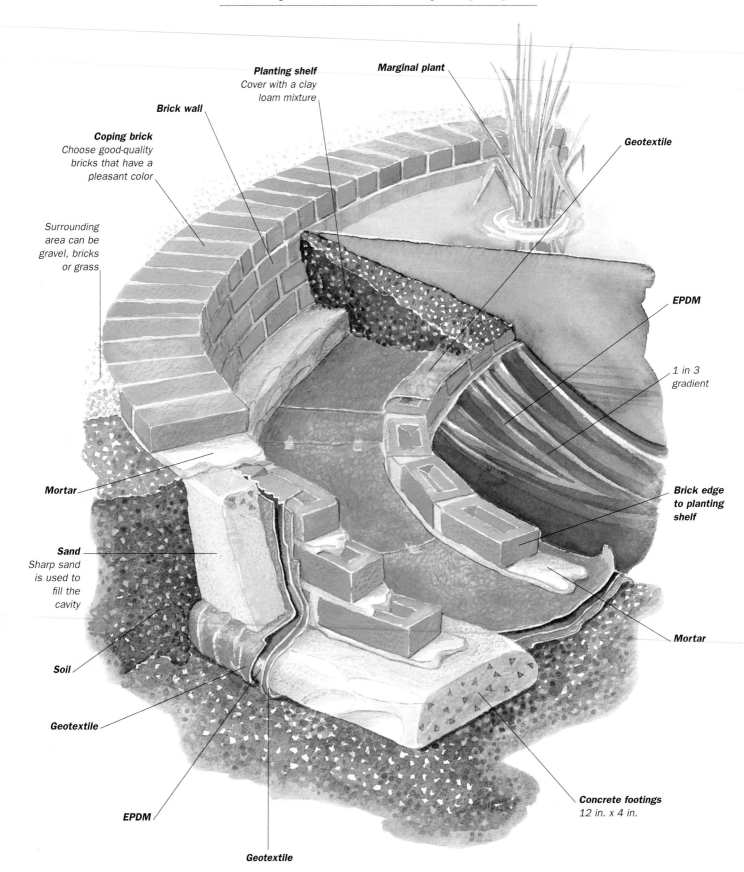

Planting shelf
Cover with a clay loam mixture

Marginal plant

Brick wall

Coping brick
Choose good-quality bricks that have a pleasant color

Geotextile

Surrounding area can be gravel, bricks or grass

EPDM

1 in 3 gradient

Mortar

Brick edge to planting shelf

Sand
Sharp sand is used to fill the cavity

Soil

Mortar

Geotextile

EPDM

Concrete footings
12 in. x 4 in.

Geotextile

Exploded view of the kidney-shaped pond

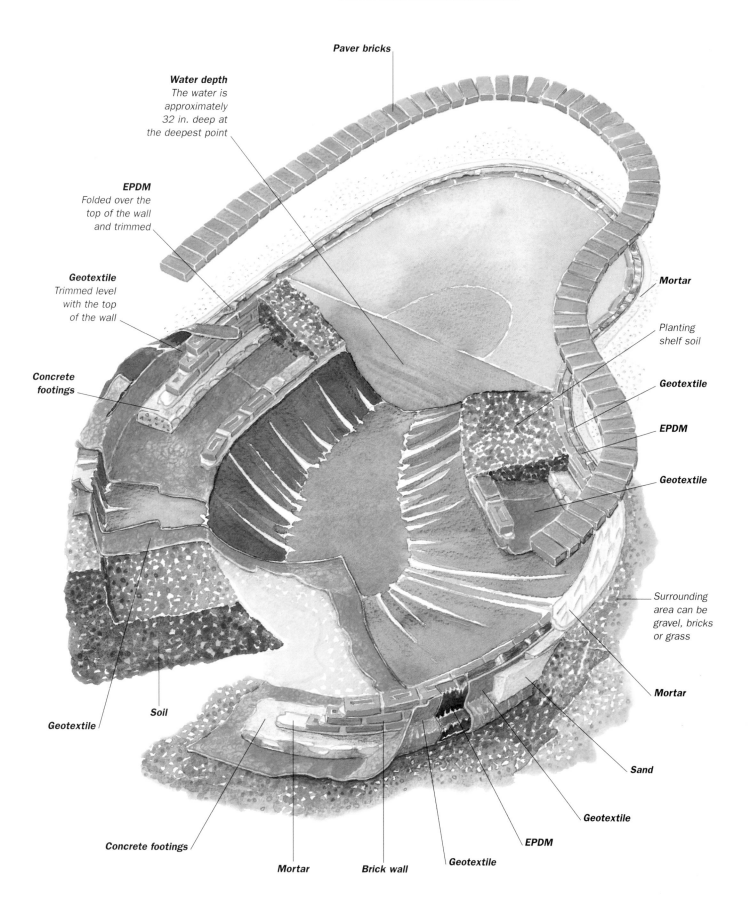

Paver bricks

Water depth
The water is approximately 32 in. deep at the deepest point

EPDM
Folded over the top of the wall and trimmed

Geotextile
Trimmed level with the top of the wall

Concrete footings

Geotextile

Soil

Geotextile

Concrete footings

Mortar

Brick wall

Geotextile

EPDM

Geotextile

Sand

Mortar

Surrounding area can be gravel, bricks or grass

Geotextile

EPDM

Geotextile

Mortar

Planting shelf soil

49

Making the kidney-shaped pond

1 Setting out the pond
Clearly mark out the area of the pond plus 1 ft. all round, marking the intended water level with a peg set outside the working area. Dig the entire area, to a level depth of 1 ft. Mark the final shape of the pond, using marker spray on the levelled ground.

2 Digging out the pond
Where planting shelves are to be built into the sides of the pond, mark out where you want them to be. Dig out the central area of the pond allowing for a 1 in 3 gradient from the marked areas. Remove any sharp stones.

3 Lining the excavation with geotextile
Unroll the geotextile (which usually comes in 6-ft. wide rolls) to cover the entire excavation allowing 4 in. overlaps. Using short lengths of duct tape join the sides of the geotextile together at 3 ft. intervals.

4 Lining the excavation with EPDM
Make sure that no stones or sharp objects have fallen into the excavation, unroll the liner and spread it ensuring that at least 1 ft. of liner overlaps the edge of the pond all around. Avoid treading on the liner.

5 Protecting the liner
Where the liner will come into direct contact with the concrete footings or brick-built sides of the pond, cover it with a further layer of geotextile, being careful that no stones or other objects come between the liner and the geotextile.

6 Building the footings and edges

On the flat ledge within the excavation, build a concrete footing 4 in. deep by 12 in. wide, making sure it is flat and level. Smooth the sides with a finishing trowel and leave to cure overnight. Build up the interior edge to the pond with three courses of bricks.

7 Filling the cavity

Gently fold the liner and geotextile over the top of the brick edging and fill the cavity between the wall and the earth with sharp sand. Compact the sand with your feet to avoid later subsidence. Do not try compacting the sand with sharp tools.

8 Preparing the planting shelves

Where the level shelf has been extended into the pond to create a planting shelf, lay a single course of bricks bedded in mortar to keep the soil from falling into the bottom of the pond. Fill the planting area with soil – a clay loam mixture is ideal.

9 Trimming the lining

Cut away the visible edges of the geotextile (any that pokes above the bricks). Leave 2 in. of EPDM above the bricks and cut off the remainder. Lay this on top of the bricks.

10 Laying the paver bricks

Lay the brick edging on a bed of mortar. Ensure that you trap the EPDM between the bricks and maintain even-looking gaps all around. Allow the mortar to dry for a few days before filling with water.

Circular pond

Filled with submerged and floating-leaf plants and their attendant wildlife, this unobtrusive, classical shape adds wonderful mirror reflections as well as beauty and interest on both the surface of the water and below it. The paved surround is perfect for sitting on when the sun is out and allows easy access to the pond, especially when the time comes to do some maintenance work on it.

Considering the design

You may wish to build this pond as part of a patio using matching stone pavers, or it could simply stand alone where it has the appearance of a well. As with all pond projects, consider the safety of children at all times (see page 13).

Getting started

Once you have chosen a level site, mark it out with pegs and string and "live with it" for a few days so that you can be sure it is in the best place for your garden. Try to complete the excavation and lining quickly, as the unsupported sides will start to collapse if there is rain during its construction.

Overall dimensions and general notes

9 ft. square

Ideal for a small formal garden, this circular pond would look good either as an extension to an existing patio or set in a lawn. You could use real stone, paving or bricks for the surround.

The pond is 5 ft. in diameter and is surrounded by a reconstituted stone paving kit

You will need

Materials

- ✔ Paving kit: 1½ in. thick pavers forming a 9 ft. square with a 5 ft. diameter hole in the middle
- ✔ Geotextile: 45 sq. yd.
- ✔ EPDM liner: 1 piece 5 sq. yd.
- ✔ Wood: 1 piece 5 ft. long
- ✔ Concrete: 1 part cement (150 lb.), and 4 parts ballast (600 lb.)
- ✔ Bricks: 220
- ✔ Mortar: 1 part cement (100 lb.) and 3 parts sand (300 lb.)
- ✔ Builders sand: 3,300 lb.
- ✔ Gravel: ½ cu yd.

Tools

- ✔ Pegs and string
- ✔ Club hammer
- ✔ Tape measure and spray marker
- ✔ Spade, fork and shovel
- ✔ Wheelbarrow and bucket
- ✔ Scissors
- ✔ General-purpose saw
- ✔ Claw hammer
- ✔ Bricklayer's towel
- ✔ Pointing towel
- ✔ Spirit level
- ✔ Sledgehammer

Cross-section of the circular pond

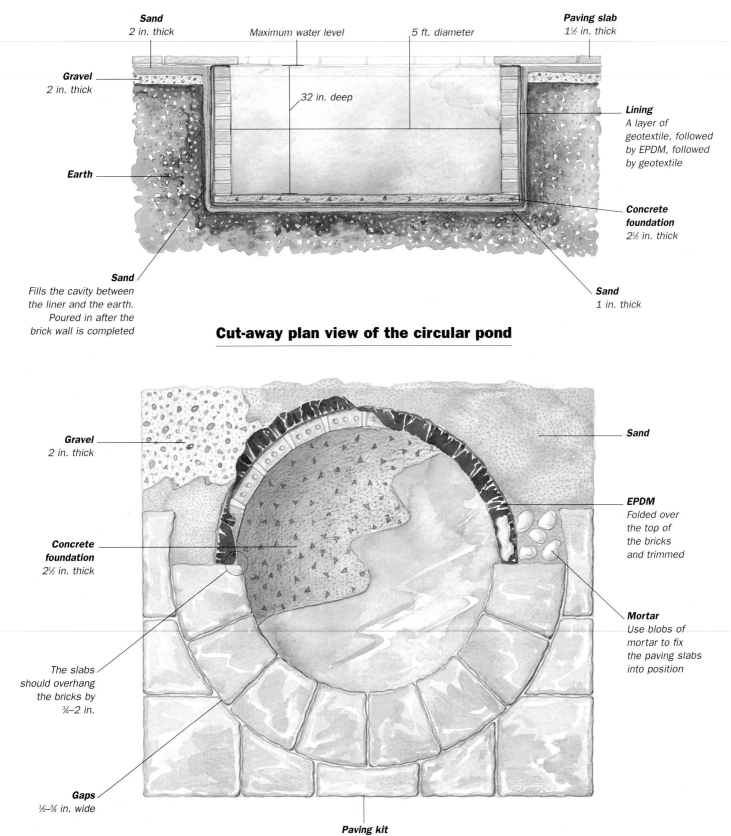

Sand
2 in. thick

Maximum water level

5 ft. diameter

Paving slab
1½ in. thick

Gravel
2 in. thick

32 in. deep

Lining
A layer of
geotextile, followed
by EPDM, followed
by geotextile

Earth

**Concrete
foundation**
2½ in. thick

Sand
Fills the cavity between
the liner and the earth.
Poured in after the
brick wall is completed

Sand
1 in. thick

Cut-away plan view of the circular pond

Gravel
2 in. thick

Sand

EPDM
Folded over
the top of
the bricks
and trimmed

**Concrete
foundation**
2½ in. thick

Mortar
Use blobs of
mortar to fix
the paving slabs
into position

The slabs
should overhang
the bricks by
¾–2 in.

Gaps
⅓–¾ in. wide

Paving kit
Approximately 9 ft. square
with a 5 ft. diameter circular hole

Exploded view of the circular pond

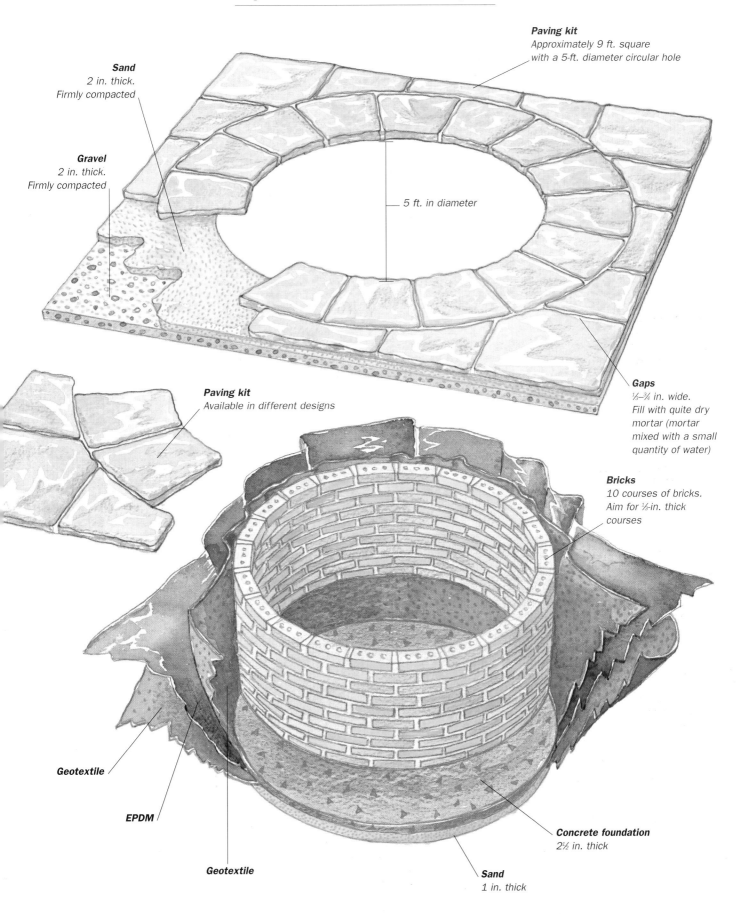

Paving kit
Approximately 9 ft. square
with a 5-ft. diameter circular hole

Sand
2 in. thick.
Firmly compacted

Gravel
2 in. thick.
Firmly compacted

5 ft. in diameter

Gaps
½–¾ in. wide.
Fill with quite dry
mortar (mortar
mixed with a small
quantity of water)

Paving kit
Available in different designs

Bricks
10 courses of bricks.
Aim for ⅓-in. thick
courses

Geotextile

EPDM

Geotextile

Concrete foundation
2½ in. thick

Sand
1 in. thick

Making the circular pond

1 Setting out the slabs

Set the paving slabs down and try them for position. Live with them for a few days. Check the dimensions of the whole square and the diameter of the circle as kits may vary slightly in size. Aim for the slabs to overhang the brick walls of the pond by ¾–2 in.

2 Marking the area

Use a tape measure, pegs, string and a spray marker to draw a circle 6 ft. in diameter. If your earth is crumbly it can be difficult to dig an accurately sized hole so start by marking out a larger circle – one 8½ ft. in diameter, for example.

3 Excavating the hole

Remove the turf with the spade and fork and start digging. You may wish to save the topsoil for another area of the garden and discard the rest. Make a hole 6 ft. in diameter and 34 in. deep, making sure it is clean-sided.

4 Lining with geotextile

Remove all sharp stones and spread a 1-in. layer of sand over the bottom of the hole. Cover the base and sides of the hole with geotextile, allowing for generous overlaps of at least 4 in. Leave it overlapping until step 11.

5 Lining with EPDM

Cover the geotextile with the 5 sq. yd. sheet of EPDM. You will find this easier if you have someone to help. Take time arranging the creases so that they end up evenly distributed and weigh down the edges with bricks. Do not put any water in at this stage.

6 Laying the concrete slab

Reline the hole with geotextile (this protects the top side of the EPDM and weigh that down with bricks. Lay a 2½-in. thick slab of concrete in the hole.

7 Positioning the brick base
Center the 5-ft. long trammel board on the concrete base, weigh it down with bricks, and use it to indicate the correct position of each brick around the circular base.

8 Building the wall
Build the circular wall with ⅓-in. thick mortar joints and stagger each course as shown. After completing each course, you can continue using the trammel by raising it upward by 3 in. each time, or you can simply check the brickwork is vertical using a spirit level.

9 Checking the levels
Check the level every two courses using the 5-ft. long board and the spirit level. Bear in mind that the pond must be completely level otherwise it will not look right. Continue building until you have completed the 10 courses.

10 Packing with sand
Use sand to fill any spaces between the sides of the hole and the geotextile. Dig out the surrounding earth down to a depth of 4 in. below the bricks. Spread 2 in. of gravel and make sure that it is firmly compacted using the sledgehammer.

11 Trimming the lining
Pack the top of the cavity with concrete. Cut the geotextile off level with the bricks. Flap the EPDM over the top of the wall and trim off the excess.

12 Putting down the paving
Spread a 2 in. layer of sand over the gravel and compact this so it finishes level with the top of the bricks. Bed the paving slabs on blobs of mortar and when that has set, fill the joints with a quite dry mortar (mixed with less water so that it is still crumbly).

Formal canal

★★
Intermediate

Making time
4 weekends
*2 weekends for
making the foundation
and 2 weekends
to complete*

This beautiful design by John Brookes is part of a formal arrangement and takes the formality of the house out into the garden. It is both simple and classic and the long strip of still water reflects the sky. The brickwork edge finishes flush with the surrounding brick, gravel and lawn, making it smart and practical. This design is easy to reduce down in size for a smaller garden or courtyard.

Considering the design

As with any formal water feature, the most important thing is to make the scheme fit the environment, so make sure that your canal allows for easy access to all areas of the garden and does not act as a "moat" to discourage use of parts of the garden. Where young children are about it is dangerous as they may crawl or walk into the canal and not be able climb out. If you have young children it is better to wait a few years for them to grow up before building a pond or if you are expecting children to visit you may consider putting up some form of temporary barrier (see page 13). In order for the water plants to flourish it is important that the depth of water is not reduced below 2 ft. It is important that the water level and the level of the patio are carefully considered so that no more steps than are necessary from the house to the pond are incorporated in the design, which is elegant and requires little maintenance.

Getting started

At nearly 16 ft. long this is a big excavation so you do need to consider where you are going to put the excavated soil. You could pay to have it removed or why not plan a rockery or other feature that requires a quantity of soil?

Overall dimensions and general notes

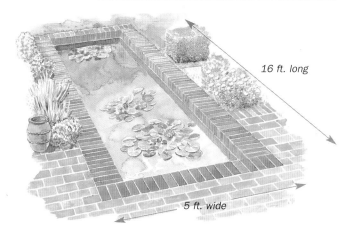

16 ft. long

5 ft. wide

This canal is suited to classic still water plants, such as water lilies.

You will need

Materials

- Gravel: 1 cu. yd.
- Concrete: 1 part cement (1,400 lb.) and 4 parts (5,600 lb.) ballast
- Blocks: 143
- Bricks: 183 for the walls and 160 for the edging
- Mortar: 1 part (200 lb.) cement and 3 parts (600 lb.) sand
- Geotextile: 72 sq. yd.
- Duct tape
- EPDM: 1 piece 25 ft. x 13 ft.

Tools

- Tape measure, pegs, string, and a piece of chalk
- Club hammer
- Spade, fork and shovel
- Sledgehammer
- General-purpose saw
- Claw hammer
- Spirit level
- Line set
- Bricklayer's trowel
- Pointing trowel

Cut-away detail of the formal canal

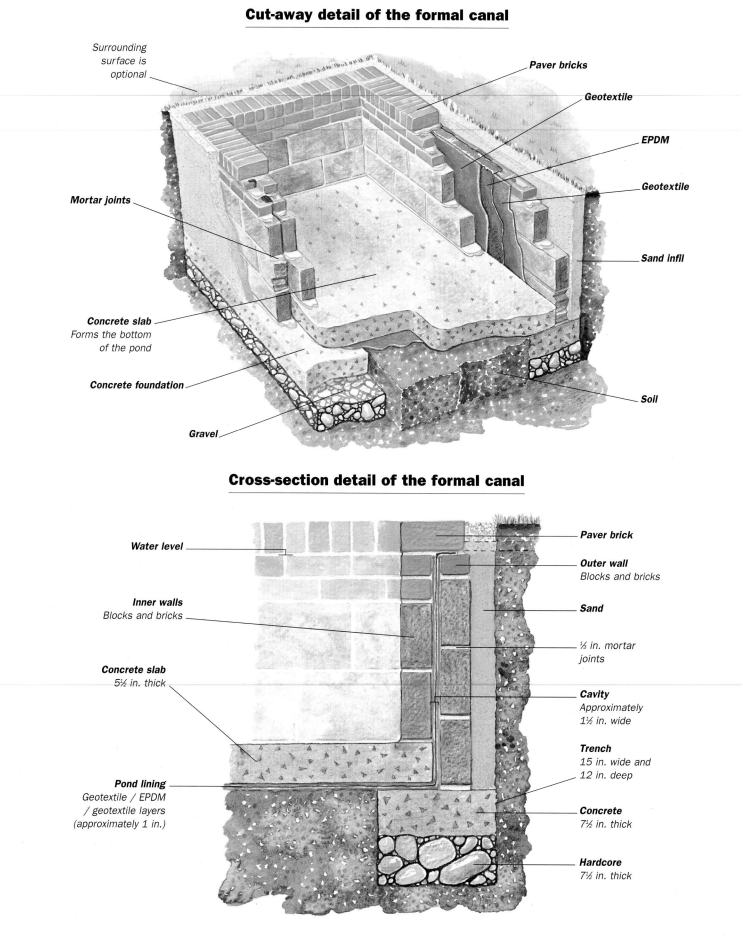

Surrounding surface is optional

Paver bricks

Geotextile

EPDM

Geotextile

Sand infil

Mortar joints

Concrete slab
Forms the bottom of the pond

Concrete foundation

Soil

Gravel

Cross-section detail of the formal canal

Water level

Inner walls
Blocks and bricks

Concrete slab
5½ in. thick

Pond lining
Geotextile / EPDM / geotextile layers (approximately 1 in.)

Paver brick

Outer wall
Blocks and bricks

Sand

⅛ in. mortar joints

Cavity
Approximately 1½ in. wide

Trench
15 in. wide and 12 in. deep

Concrete
7½ in. thick

Hardcore
7½ in. thick

Exploded view of the formal canal (paver bricks not shown)

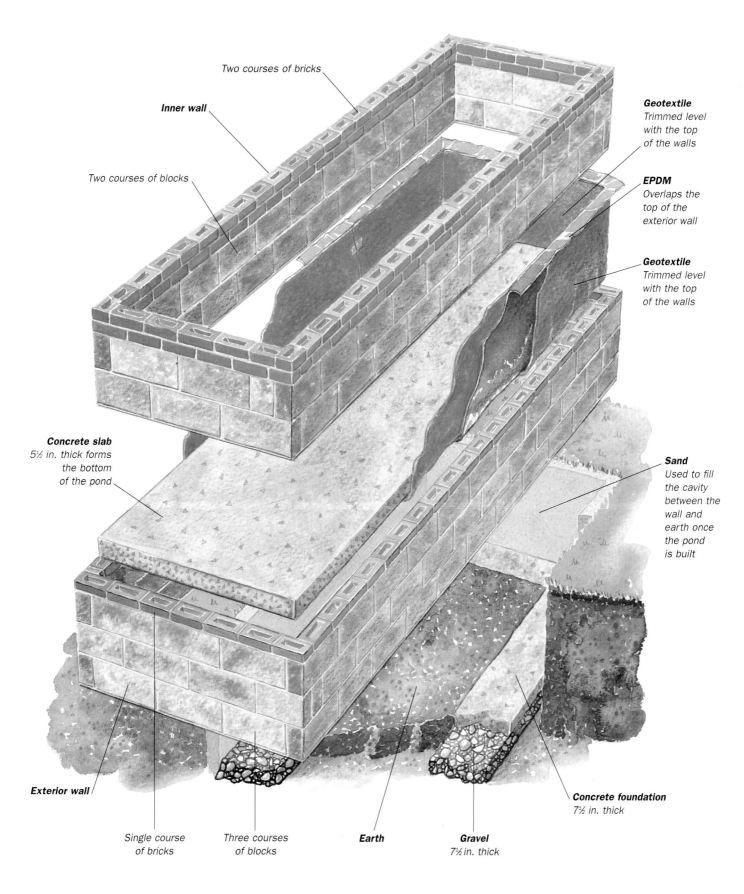

Two courses of bricks

Inner wall

Two courses of blocks

Geotextile
Trimmed level with the top of the walls

EPDM
Overlaps the top of the exterior wall

Geotextile
Trimmed level with the top of the walls

Concrete slab
5½ in. thick forms the bottom of the pond

Sand
Used to fill the cavity between the wall and earth once the pond is built

Exterior wall

Single course of bricks

Three courses of blocks

Earth

Gravel
7½ in. thick

Concrete foundation
7½ in. thick

Making the formal canal

1 Excavating the area
Clearly mark out an area 16 ft. x 5½ ft. and remove all materials in it to a depth of 34 in. Mark out a 15-in.-wide foundation trench into the bottom of the hole and remove the earth to a depth of 12 in.

2 Laying the foundation
Fill the trench with gravel to a depth of 7½ in. Use pegs and wood to form a level frame and fill this with concrete. Screed the concrete level with the frame using a piece of spare wood. Leave to set overnight.

3 Building the exterior wall
Remove the wood frame and mark out the position of the outside edge of the exterior wall on the concrete using the chalk (16 ft. x 5 ft.).

4 Lining with geotextile
Carefully line the entire area with geotextile right to the top, folding or cutting away the darts that are formed at the corners. Use duct tape to join the pieces together.

5 Lining with EPDM
Place the EPDM liner into the lined area, ensuring the sides reach the top all round. Use bricks wrapped in geotextile to push the liner into the corners, fold and tape the darts that rise from each corner. Cut away the liner 4 in. above the top of the bricks.

6 Laying the concrete slab
Reline the hole with more geotextile. Make a screed frame from spare wood and use it to cover the bottom of the hole with a level layer of concrete about $5\frac{1}{2}$ in. deep. Allow to dry overnight.

7 Building the inner wall
Use the chalk to mark out the inside edge of the inner wall ($14\frac{3}{4}$ ft. x $3\frac{1}{2}$ ft.). This leaves a cavity of about 1 in. to accommodate the lining. Build up two courses of blocks followed by two courses of bricks.

8 Putting on the coping bricks
Trim the geotextile layers level with the top of the cavity wall and weigh down the EPDM so that it overlaps the top of the exterior wall. Lay paver bricks on a bed of mortar and finish by filling the cavity between the wall and the earth with sand.

Pond with bridge and beach

★ ★
Intermediate

**Making time
4 weekends**
*2 weekends for
digging the hole
and 2 weekends
for finishing*

An informal wildlife pond provides interest all year round and fascinates children and adults alike. A wide range of pond life quickly grows up and newts, frogs and toads often appear as if by magic. A natural-looking beach and imaginative planting with lilies, iris and primroses complete the picture. The simple plank bridge gives a sense of adventure and can also save you walking all the way around the pond!

Overall dimensions and general notes

A 13-ft. long bridge spans the narrowest point of the pond

The pond is approximately 26 ft. long and 16 ft. wide

The best all-round advice is to go for the biggest pond that money, time and space allows.

An area of natural-looking beach

Considering the design

This pond can be built anywhere in the garden and is often away from the house in a quiet spot with wild flower and native species planting. It is often appropriate to put a bench or seat nearby for quiet contemplation. Be sure to make it as large as possible as plant growth on the water will soon make it appear smaller than it actually is. Make sure that you leave a clear area on one side so that you can walk up to it and see it clearly. People will be drawn to it if they can see a reflection or shimmer from the house. A pebble "beach" provides an attractive edge to the pond (see inset). As always, consider child safety (see page 13).

Getting started

See if you can find a place to put the earth from the excavations elsewhere in the garden (build a rockery for example), as this can be expensive to remove.

You will need

Materials

- Geotextile: 138 sq. yd.
- Duct tape
- EPDM: 1 piece 36 ft. x 26 ft.
- Concrete: 1 part cement (990 lb.) and 4 parts ballast (3,960 lb.)
- Bricks: 315
- Mortar: 1 part cement (110 lb.) and 3 parts sand (330 lb.)
- Wood: 3 pieces, 4 in. x 4 in. x 19 in. (bridge frame horizontals), 6 pieces 4 in. x 4 in. x 27½ in. (bridge frame verticals), 2 pieces (natural irregular edge is optional) 2 in. x 10–12 in. x 13 ft. (bridge planks)
- Bolts: 12 at 4 in. x ½ in. each with 1 nut and 2 washers, galvanised (bridge frames)
- Nails: 12 at 5 in. long, galvanised flat headed
- Sand: 1,550 lb.

Tools

- Tape measure, hosepipe or rope (100 ft. long, for marking pond shape), spray marker and peg
- Club hammer and claw hammer
- Spade, fork and shovel
- Wheelbarrow and bucket
- Spirit level
- Rake
- Scissors
- Bricklayer's trowel and pointing trowel
- General-purpose saw
- Drill and ½-in. diameter bit

Cross-section detail of the bridge

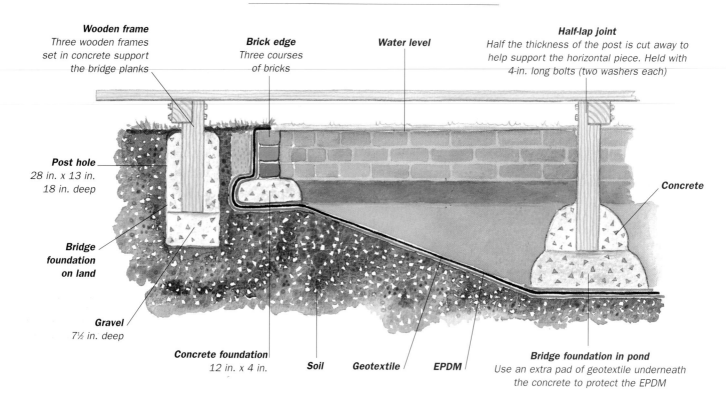

Wooden frame
*Three wooden frames
set in concrete support
the bridge planks*

Brick edge
*Three courses
of bricks*

Water level

Half-lap joint
*Half the thickness of the post is cut away to
help support the horizontal piece. Held with
4-in. long bolts (two washers each)*

Post hole
*28 in. x 13 in.
18 in. deep*

Concrete

**Bridge
foundation
on land**

Gravel
7½ in. deep

Concrete foundation
12 in. x 4 in.

Soil   **Geotextile**   **EPDM**

Bridge foundation in pond
*Use an extra pad of geotextile underneath
the concrete to protect the EPDM*

Cross-section detail of the pond showing beach (bridge not shown)

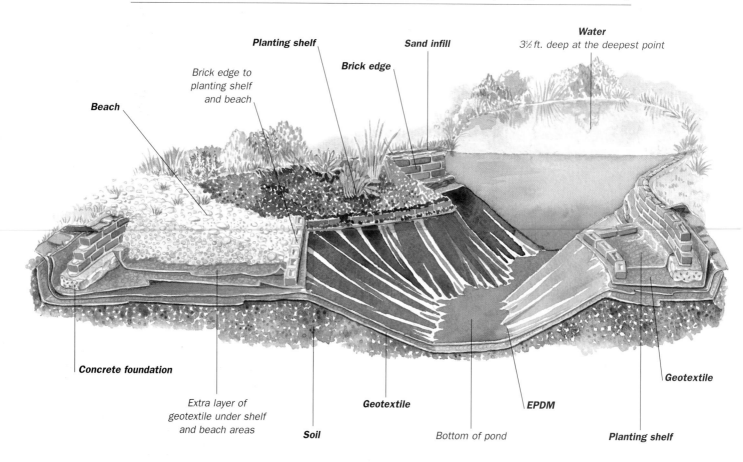

Planting shelf

Brick edge

Sand infill

Water
3½ ft. deep at the deepest point

*Brick edge to
planting shelf
and beach*

Beach

Concrete foundation

*Extra layer of
geotextile under shelf
and beach areas*

Soil

Geotextile

EPDM

Geotextile

Bottom of pond

Planting shelf

Exploded view of the pond with bridge and beach

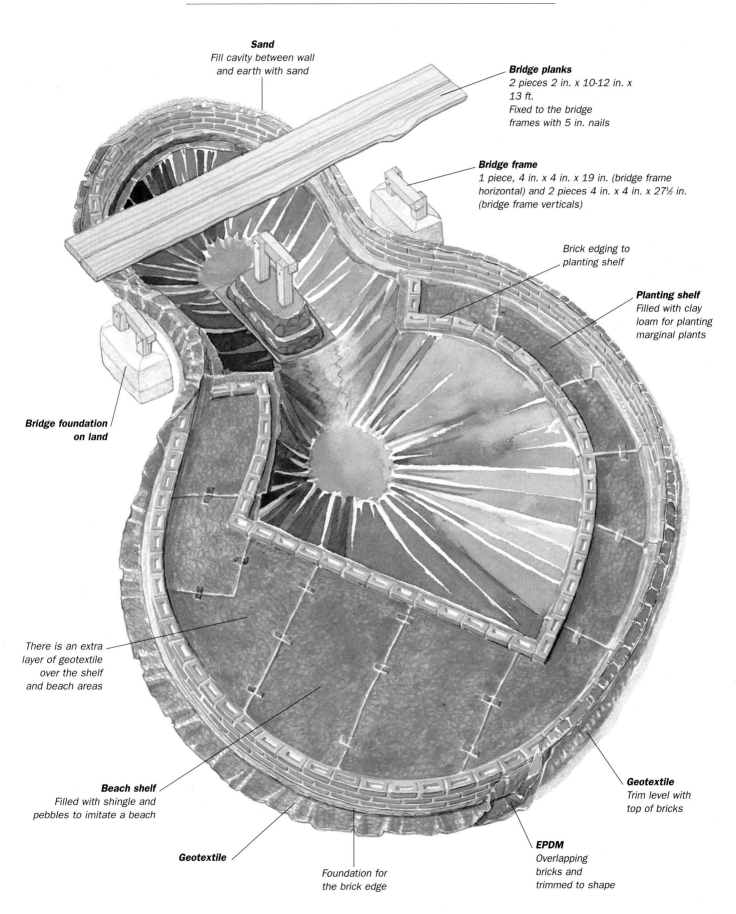

Sand
Fill cavity between wall and earth with sand

Bridge planks
2 pieces 2 in. x 10-12 in. x 13 ft.
Fixed to the bridge frames with 5 in. nails

Bridge frame
1 piece, 4 in. x 4 in. x 19 in. (bridge frame horizontal) and 2 pieces 4 in. x 4 in. x 27½ in. (bridge frame verticals)

Brick edging to planting shelf

Planting shelf
Filled with clay loam for planting marginal plants

Bridge foundation on land

There is an extra layer of geotextile over the shelf and beach areas

Geotextile
Trim level with top of bricks

Beach shelf
Filled with shingle and pebbles to imitate a beach

Geotextile

Foundation for the brick edge

EPDM
Overlapping bricks and trimmed to shape

Making the pond with bridge and beach

1 Excavating the area
Mark out the area of the pond. Near the pond but outside the workings drive in a wooden marker peg so the top is at the intended water level. Dig the area to 1 ft. below that level and mark out planting shelf areas. Dig out the remaining earth to finish the hole.

2 Measuring and raking
Allow at least 1 ft. extra on both length and width. Rake over the excavation removing any sharp objects which could damage the liner.

3 Lining the excavation
Cover the entire excavation with geotextile, allowing for 4 in. overlaps. Spread the EPDM over the geotextile ensuring that it extends beyond the water level all round when the pond is filled. Rearrange creases so that they are distributed evenly.

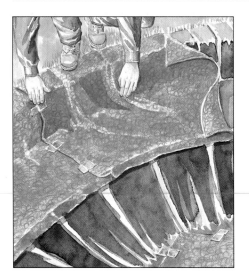

4 Laying extra geotextile
Make sure that no stones or sharp objects have fallen into the excavation and then lay extra geotextile over the planting shelf and beach areas. Use short lengths of duct tape to join the 3 ft. wide sheets of geotextile.

5 Building the footings and edges
On the flat ledge within the excavation build a concrete footing 4 in. deep by 12 in. wide, ensuring it is level and flat. Smooth all the sides with a finishing trowel and leave to cure overnight. Build up the interior edge to the pond with 3 courses of bricks.

6 Building the bridge frames
Establish the finished height of your bridge and prepare the bridge frame components accordingly. Mold a concrete pad for supporting the central frame. Hold it upright while you spread a mound of concrete around the bottoms of the wooden posts.

7 Completing the bridge

Dig holes either side of the pond and set the other two frames in concrete so that they are vertical and also levelled and aligned with the central frame. Once the concrete has set, fix the bridge planks to the tops of the frames using nails.

8 Backfilling behind the lining

The geotextile needs to be trimmed level with the top of the bricks and the EPDM should overlap the bricks and then be trimmed. Fill the cavity behind the wall with sand. Compact the sand with your feet to avoid later subsidence but take care to avoid damaging the liner.

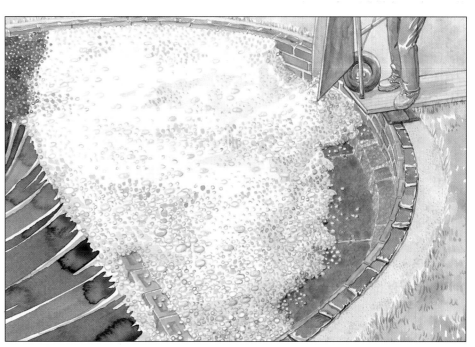

9 Preparing the planting shelves

Where the level shelf has been extended into the pond to create a planting shelf, check that you have adequate geotextile protecting the EPDM and then lay a line of bricks along the edge (mortar is not required). Fill the planting shelves with clay loam.

10 Creating the beach and finishing the pond

Fill the beach area with a mixture of shingle and differently sized pebbles. Use a board to protect the edge of the pond while you work. When the pond is filled with water, cover the tops of the bricks with turf, cutting the turf at the edge of the water. Alternatively, cover with soil and sow grass seed.

Raised pond

★ ★
Intermediate

Making time
4 weekends
*A weekend to make
the foundation and
3 weekends for
completion*

Ideal for a small garden or patio area, the edging allows for seating close to the water where you can see into the water as well as looking at the reflections of the sky and seasons. It is adaptable and takes up little space and, where there are children around it is safer, as they are less likely to stumble into the water. Placed where it can be seen from the house, it will give interest and delight throughout the year.

Considering the design

This little pond can be square or rectangular in shape and should be as large as possible, allowing for access around the area. The edging stone is 21 in. above the ground and this is just about low enough to make a comfortable seating place. Place it where it can be seen from inside the house from a much-used vantage point. Use materials that closely match those that form your house. Consider the reflections that you will see from your vantage point; placing a mirror (horizontally) where the water level will ultimately be will give you a

good idea of the end result. Consider any services (water, drainage, TV, electricity, gas, or sewerage) that may be underneath the proposed site and alter the scheme accordingly. Note how the pond butts against the wall; a good option if you are short of space.

Getting started

Make a drawing showing the size that you have chosen. Use this to order the material that you will want. Allow 10% over on all materials. If materials have to be carried through the house remove or protect vulnerable things.

You will need

Materials

- ✔ Concrete: 1 part cement (65 lb.) and 4 parts ballast (260 lb.)
- ✔ Wood: 5 ft. x 1 in. x 3 in. (tamping beam)
- ✔ Bricks: 196 bricks and 180 handmade irregular bricks (approximately 9 in. x 4 in. x 2½ in.)
- ✔ Mortar mix: 1 part cement (165 lb.) and 3 parts sand (495 lb.)
- ✔ Rigid liner: 6 ft. x 4½ ft. (at outer rim) and 20 in. deep
- ✔ Stone slabs: 22 tiles, 11½ in. square and 1 in. thick

Tools

- ✔ Tape measure, pegs, string and a piece of chalk
- ✔ Club hammer
- ✔ Spade, fork and shovel
- ✔ Wheelbarrow and bucket
- ✔ Spirit level
- ✔ Line set
- ✔ Bricklayer's trowel and pointing trowel
- ✔ Angle grinder

Overall dimensions and general notes

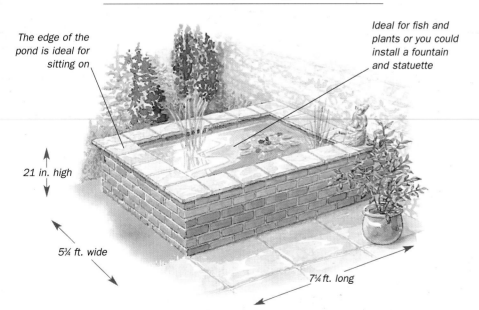

The edge of the pond is ideal for sitting on

Ideal for fish and plants or you could install a fountain and statuette

21 in. high

5¾ ft. wide

7¼ ft. long

This pond structure is built around a pre-formed rigid liner, so purchase the liner to suit your space first, and then adjust the material quantities accordingly.

Plan view of the raised pond showing first courses of brick wall

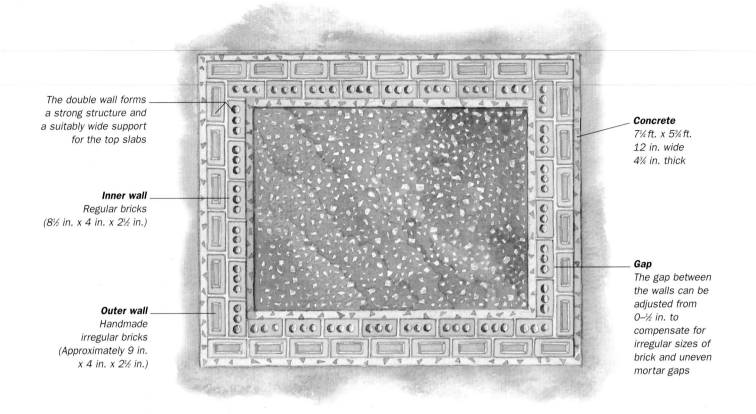

The double wall forms a strong structure and a suitably wide support for the top slabs

Inner wall
*Regular bricks
(8½ in. x 4 in. x 2½ in.)*

Outer wall
*Handmade
irregular bricks
(Approximately 9 in.
x 4 in. x 2½ in.)*

Concrete
*7¼ ft. x 5¾ ft.
12 in. wide
4¾ in. thick*

Gap
*The gap between
the walls can be
adjusted from
0–½ in. to
compensate for
irregular sizes of
brick and uneven
mortar gaps*

Cross-section of the raised pond

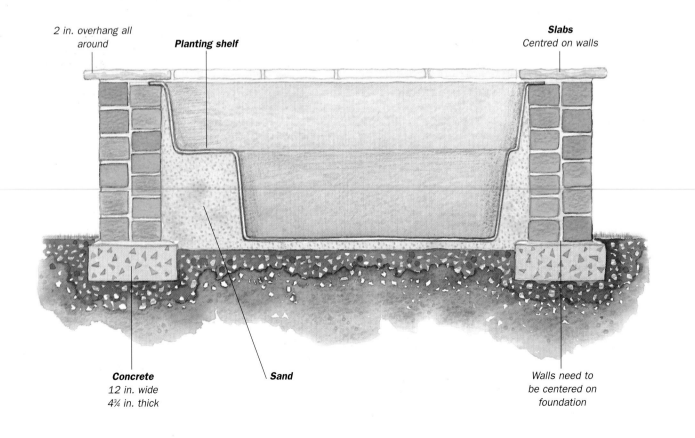

*2 in. overhang all
around*

Planting shelf

Slabs
Centred on walls

Concrete
*12 in. wide
4¾ in. thick*

Sand

*Walls need to
be centered on
foundation*

Exploded view of the raised pond

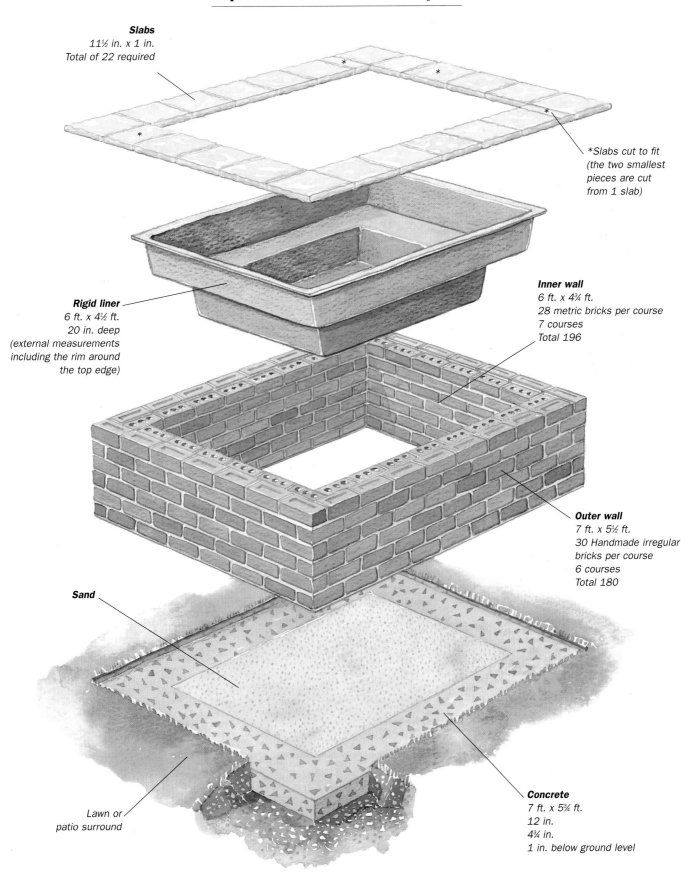

Slabs
11½ in. x 1 in.
Total of 22 required

*Slabs cut to fit
(the two smallest
pieces are cut
from 1 slab)

Inner wall
6 ft. x 4¾ ft.
28 metric bricks per course
7 courses
Total 196

Rigid liner
6 ft. x 4½ ft.
20 in. deep
(external measurements
including the rim around
the top edge)

Outer wall
7 ft. x 5½ ft.
30 Handmade irregular
bricks per course
6 courses
Total 180

Sand

Concrete
7 ft. x 5¾ ft.
12 in.
4¾ in.
1 in. below ground level

Lawn or
patio surround

Making the raised pond

1 Marking out
Using the tape measure, pegs and string, set out the shape of the foundation on the grass – 7 ft. long and 5¾ ft. wide. Remove the turf.

2 Positioning the levelling pegs
Dig out the foundation trench, 12 in. wide and 6 in. deep. Hammer in a series of wooden pegs to establish a level about 1 in. lower than the lawn.

3 Screeding the concrete
Fill the foundation trench with concrete up to the level of the wooden pegs. (Note the workboard to protect the lawn.)

4 Practice laying the bricks
Set out the first course of bricks without using mortar so that you can see how the pattern works. Arrange the ordinary bricks on the inside and the larger handmade bricks on the outside. Try to avoid cutting bricks.

5 Building the walls
Build up the inside walls to a height of six courses, and check both the vertical and horizontal levels. Use the line set to help you lay the bricks in accurate straight lines.

6 Fitting the rigid liner

Sit the plastic liner in the brick box so that the rim is resting on top of the wall. Fill the cavity between the liner and the wall with sand. Avoid leaving any gaps as these can cause the liner to distort or break over time (see page 26).

7 Cleaning the mortar joints

Build up the outside wall at the corners so that the top course is slightly higher than the level of the inner wall. Use the handle of the trowel to rake the courses to a clean finish while the mortar is still workable.

8 Finishing the brickwork

Continue laying up the courses until you have finished the exterior wall. Keep checking with the spirit level and making adjustments as necessary.

9 Laying the coping slabs

Practice arranging the slabs around the top of the pond allowing for a 2 in. overhang all around. Try to avoid cutting slabs where possible. Trowel a generous layer of mortar on top of the walls and bed the coping slabs in place. Check that they are level.

Pond with decking

★ ★ ★

Advanced

Making time
4-weekends
*A weekend for
digging the hole and
2 weekends for
construction*

**Decking over a pond invites you to step over the water on to a different world.
To look down in the gaps between the boards adds to the sense of adventure like being
on a pleasure pier, a boat or raft. A railing is a good idea – made from metal or wood –
and will stop young children falling in and will give you somewhere to rest your elbows
and feel secure while looking down into the pond and observing the wildlife.**

Considering the design

Decking can disguise the point at which
the land stops and the pond starts so this
combination has a lot of potential. You
can alter the size and shape of the decking to suit your requirements.

The deck boards need to be strong
and resistant to rotting. Preserved pine
(stained or painted) is suitable but
untreated bare oak is even better. If you
have railings, they need to be strong, well
supported and about 3 ft. high.

Getting started

If you require a deck of a different size
and shape or are working with an existing
pond, start by planning it out on paper.

Overall dimensions and general notes

Decking boards
made from
preserved pine
or bare oak

An irregular
shaped pond
with a natural-
looking edge,
17½ ft. x 11½ ft.

7½ ft. wide

11 ft. long

*The size and shape of the decking can be altered to suit your needs but be sure to
provide adequate supports. Wood or metal railing is a sensible option.*

You will need

Materials

- Geotextile: 65 sq. yd.
- Duct tape
- EPDM: 1 piece 23 ft. x 20 ft.
- Concrete: 1 part cement (500 lb.)
  and 4 parts (2,000 lb.) ballast
- Bricks: 210
- Mortar: 1 part cement (85 lb.) and
  3 parts sand (255 lb.)
- Sand: 880 lb.
- Gravel: 3½ cu. ft.
- Tanking paint: 1 gal.

- Wood: 10 pieces, 4 in. x 4 in. x 14 in.
  (posts), 2 pieces 4 in. x 4 in. x 7 ft.
  (deck frame horizontals, long), 2
  pieces 4 in. x 4 in. x 4 ft. (deck frame
  horizontals, short), 6 pieces 2 in. x
  8 in. x 11 ft. (deck boards, long) and 5
  pieces 2 in. x 8 in. x 4½ ft. (deck
  boards, short)
- Bolts: 20 at ½ in. x 7 in. each with 1
  nut and 2 washers, galvanised
- Nails: 68 at 5 in. long, galvanised

Tools

- Tape measure, rope or hose (for

marking shape of pond), peg and
spray marker
- Spade, fork and shovel
- Spirit level
- Scissors
- Bricklayer's trowel and pointing
  trowel
- General-purpose saw
- Wrench (to fit nuts)
- Claw hammer

Exploded view of the pond with decking

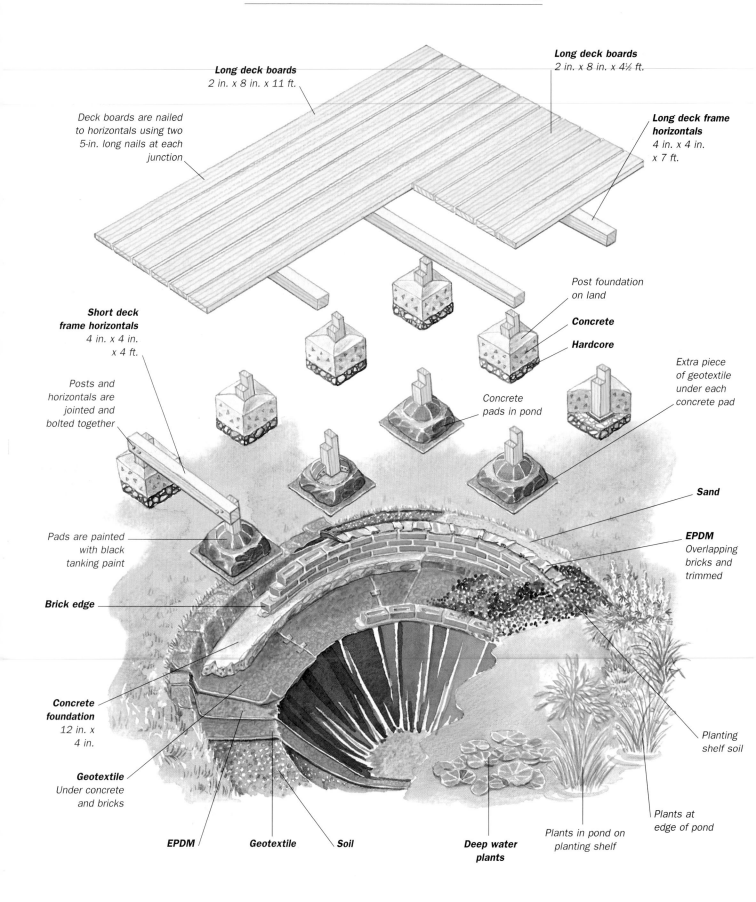

Long deck boards
2 in. x 8 in. x 11 ft.

Long deck boards
2 in. x 8 in. x 4½ ft.

Deck boards are nailed
to horizontals using two
5-in. long nails at each
junction

**Long deck frame
horizontals**
4 in. x 4 in.
x 7 ft.

**Short deck
frame horizontals**
4 in. x 4 in.
x 4 ft.

Post foundation
on land

Concrete

Hardcore

Extra piece
of geotextile
under each
concrete pad

Posts and
horizontals are
jointed and
bolted together

Concrete
pads in pond

Sand

EPDM
Overlapping
bricks and
trimmed

Pads are painted
with black
tanking paint

Brick edge

**Concrete
foundation**
12 in. x
4 in.

Planting
shelf soil

Geotextile
Under concrete
and bricks

Plants at
edge of pond

EPDM   **Geotextile**   **Soil**

**Deep water
plants**

Plants in pond on
planting shelf

Cut-away detail of the pond with decking

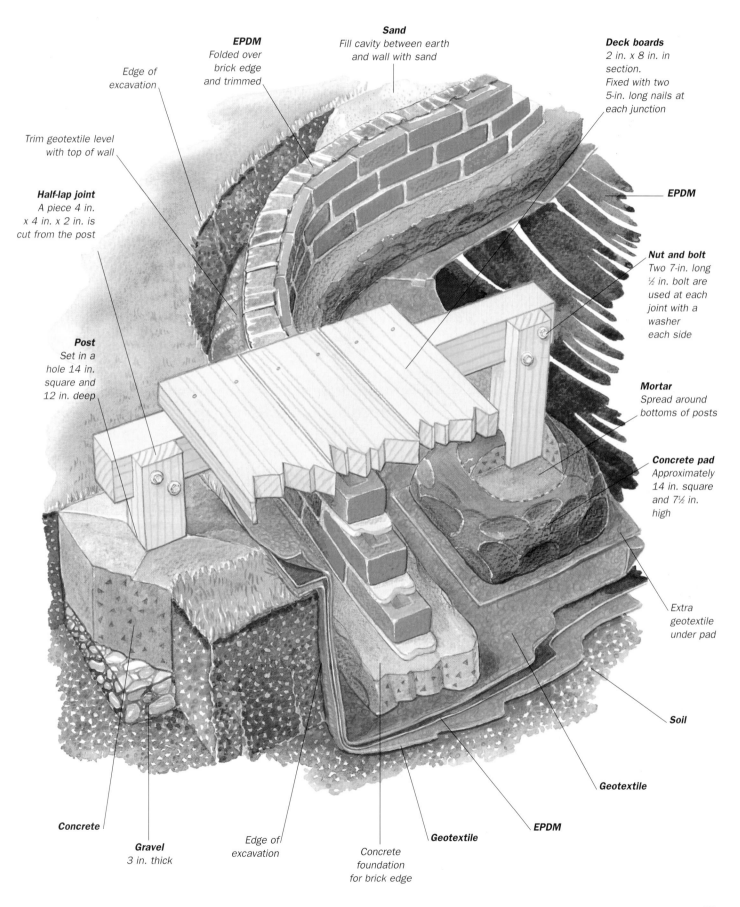

EPDM
Folded over brick edge and trimmed

Sand
Fill cavity between earth and wall with sand

Deck boards
2 in. x 8 in. in section.
Fixed with two 5-in. long nails at each junction

Edge of excavation

Trim geotextile level with top of wall

Half-lap joint
A piece 4 in. x 4 in. x 2 in. is cut from the post

EPDM

Nut and bolt
Two 7-in. long ½ in. bolt are used at each joint with a washer each side

Post
Set in a hole 14 in. square and 12 in. deep

Mortar
Spread around bottoms of posts

Concrete pad
Approximately 14 in. square and 7½ in. high

Extra geotextile under pad

Soil

Geotextile

Concrete

Gravel
3 in. thick

Edge of excavation

Concrete foundation for brick edge

Geotextile

EPDM

Making the pond with decking

1 Marking out and excavating
Clearly mark out the area of the pond plus 12 in. all round and dig to a depth of 14 in. Mark out the final shape of the pond. Where planting shelves are to be built in to the sides of the pond, mark out the shelves and then finish digging out the pond.

2 Lining the pond
Remove any sharp objects from the hole. Cover the entire excavation with geotextile allowing 4 in. overlaps. Use duct tape to join the sides together at 3 ft. intervals. Unroll the EPDM liner and lay it over the area, ensuring it extends beyond the intended water level.

3 Building the footing
Protect the liner with another layer of geotextile on the shelf areas. On the flat ledge within the excavation build a concrete footing 4 in. deep by 12 in. wide ensuring it is level and flat. Smooth all the sides with a finishing trowel and leave to cure overnight.

4 Building the edges
Build the interior edge to the pond with 3 courses of bricks. Check the horizontal level with the spirit level. Clean the wall with the edge of the trowel so that it is free from sharp bits of mortar.

5 Making the planting shelves
Fill the area behind the wall with sand, compact it with your feet to avoid later subsidence and trim the geotextile and EPDM. Lay bricks along the edge of the planting shelves and fill these recesses with soil for planting.

7 Finishing the deck frame

Fix the horizontal framework to the posts at the side of the pond so that they are all level with each other. Cut the remaining posts to length, rest them on the concrete pads and bolt them to the horizontals.

6 Locating the deck posts

Establish where the deck posts need to be. For those to the side of the pond dig holes and set them in concrete, and for the ones in the pond make up concrete pads 14 in. square and 7½ in. deep. Position on top of an extra layer of geotextile.

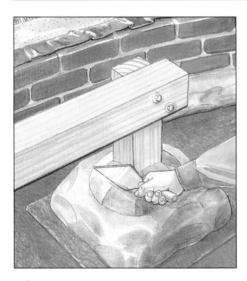

8 Supporting with mortar

Ensure that the posts on the concrete pads are supported with mortar to stop any possible horizontal movement. Trowel the mortar to a smooth finish. Once set, paint the pads with black tanking paint.

9 Fixing the deck boards and completing the pond

Carefully nail on the decking boards using the strip of plywood to set gaps of ¼ in. and two nails at each junction. Cover the brick wall and exposed edge of the lining with turf or soil and plant grass seed.

Mosaic pond

Ideal for a small garden or courtyard, this elegant circular fountain pond will both cool the air and make the music of water. Its timeless, classical shape will fit in any outdoor room. The mosaic design is a special touch that adds style to your water feature and gives you the opportunity to be creative; if you don't like the fish shapes, look for other images, colors, shapes and patterns that inspire you.

Making time
3 weekends
A weekend for making the foundation and 2 weekends to complete

Considering the design

The only limiting factor in this design is the size of the plastic sump. Make sure that you can get one the right size. If you want to keep the mosaic bright, you will need to keep the water sparkling and sterile. Use bromine tablets available from a swimming pool supply company. As always, consider child safety (see page 13).

Getting started

Once you have decided where to site the pond, consider how you are going to get electrical power to it. You are creating a work of art so do not hurry – enjoy it.

Overall dimensions and general notes

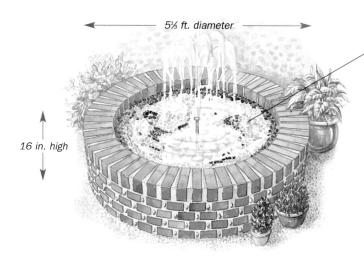

5⅓ ft. diameter

16 in. high

Lined with concrete and covered in a bold mosaic design

The pond can be increased in size but it should not be made any smaller, as the joints between the bricks become too wide.

You will need

Materials

- ✔ Wood: 2 pieces ¾ in. x 3 in. x 5¾ ft., 2 pieces ¾ in. x 3 in. x 5½ ft., 4 pieces ¾ in. x 3 in. x 27½ in., 2 pieces ¾ in. x 3 in. x 21¼ in. and 2 pieces ¾ in. x 3 in. x 20 in. (for the formwork), 1 piece 26 in. long (tramel arm), 1 piece 3 in. x 7½ in. (tramel block)
- ✔ Nails: 36 at 2¾ in. long
- ✔ Concrete: 1 part cement (220 lb.) and 4 parts ballast (880 lb.)
- ✔ Plywood: 1 piece ¼ in. x 24 in. x 24 in. (trammel base) and 1 piece ⅓ in. x 24 in. x 4½ ft. (concrete former)
- ✔ Bricks: 192

- ✔ Mortar: 1 part cement (110 lb.) and 3 parts sand (330 lb.)
- ✔ Cobbles: 140 for decorating the wall and 220 lb. to fill the sump
- ✔ Rigid plastic sump: 3 ft. in diameter (15 in. diameter sump) and 7 in. deep
- ✔ EPDM: 1 piece 2¾ sq. yd.
- ✔ Plastic pipe (length to suit your site)
- ✔ Duct tape
- ✔ Thin card: 1 piece
- ✔ Glazed tiles: 30, in an assortment of colours (see page 85)
- ✔ Waterproof tile cement and grout
- ✔ Pump

Tools

- ✔ Tape measure, pegs, string, piece of chalk and a spirit level
- ✔ Club hammer and claw hammer
- ✔ Spade and shovel
- ✔ Wheelbarrow and bucket
- ✔ General-purpose saw and hacksaw
- ✔ Bricklayer's towel and pointing trowel
- ✔ Scissors
- ✔ Brick hammer
- ✔ Jigsaw

Plan view showing foundation formwork and method of laying bricks

Cut-away plan view (before concrete is applied)

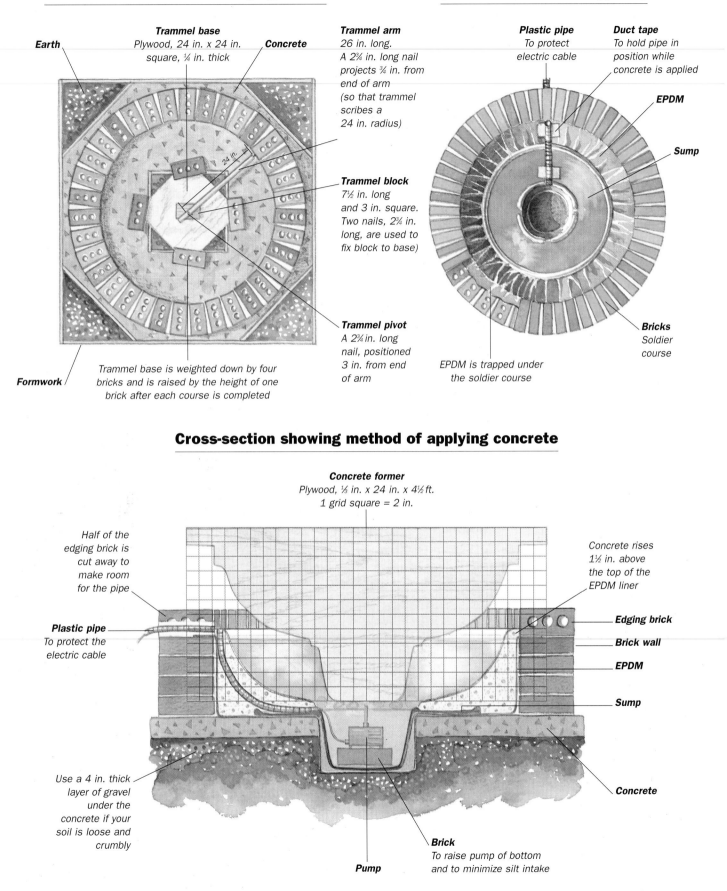

Earth

Trammel base
Plywood, 24 in. x 24 in. square, ¼ in. thick

Concrete

Trammel arm
26 in. long.
A 2¾ in. long nail projects ¾ in. from end of arm (so that trammel scribes a 24 in. radius)

24 in.

Trammel block
7½ in. long and 3 in. square. Two nails, 2¾ in. long, are used to fix block to base)

Trammel pivot
A 2¾ in. long nail, positioned 3 in. from end of arm

Formwork

Trammel base is weighted down by four bricks and is raised by the height of one brick after each course is completed

Plastic pipe
To protect electric cable

Duct tape
To hold pipe in position while concrete is applied

EPDM

Sump

Bricks
Soldier course

EPDM is trapped under the soldier course

Cross-section showing method of applying concrete

Concrete former
Plywood, ⅛ in. x 24 in. x 4½ ft.
1 grid square = 2 in.

Half of the edging brick is cut away to make room for the pipe

Concrete rises 1½ in. above the top of the EPDM liner

Plastic pipe
To protect the electric cable

Edging brick

Brick wall

EPDM

Sump

Use a 4 in. thick layer of gravel under the concrete if your soil is loose and crumbly

Concrete

Brick
To raise pump of bottom and to minimize silt intake

Pump

Exploded view of the mosaic pond

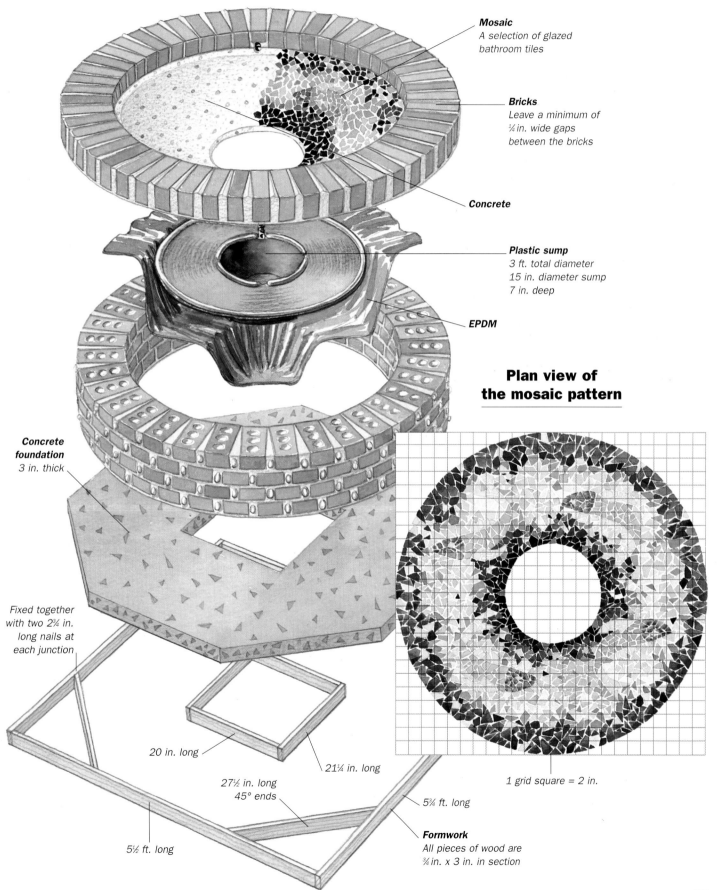

Mosaic
A selection of glazed bathroom tiles

Bricks
Leave a minimum of ¼ in. wide gaps between the bricks

Concrete

Plastic sump
3 ft. total diameter
15 in. diameter sump
7 in. deep

EPDM

Plan view of the mosaic pattern

Concrete foundation
3 in. thick

Fixed together with two 2¾ in. long nails at each junction

20 in. long

21¼ in. long

27½ in. long
45° ends

5½ ft. long

5¾ ft. long

Formwork
All pieces of wood are
¾ in. x 3 in. in section

1 grid square = 2 in.

Making the mosaic pond

1 Laying the concrete

Cut the ¾ in. x 3 in. wood to size and build the formwork. Dig out the foundation to a depth of 8 in., set the formwork in place and check it is horizontal using the spirit level. Pour in concrete and screed it level with the top of the frame using an offcut.

2 Setting out the first course

Build the trammel so that it scribes a 2 ft. radius and use this to help you position the bricks. Bed the bricks on mortar, and check them with the spirit level. Build three more staggered courses of brick raising the trammel for each course.

4 Putting in the sump

Dig the earth out from the center of the foundation slab and set the plastic sump in place to make sure it fits.

3 Placing the decorative cobbles

Fill each of the angled joints with mortar and decorate with cobbles. Carefully select the cobbles for best effect.

5 Fitting the EPDM
Remove the plastic sump, drape the EPDM over the whole pond and arrange it so that the folds are evenly distributed. Replace the sump and trim the EPDM ensuring you leave a generous overlap on top of the wall.

6 Laying the bricks
Lay the top layer of soldier bricks (the edging) around the edge of the pond using the trammel to guide you. Take extra care to space the bricks evenly and check each one is horizontal using the spirit level. Leave out one of the bricks at the back (see step 7).

7 Fitting the pipe
Lay a short length of pipe for taking the electric cable under the last brick of the soldier course (cut the brick in half). Run more pipe from the edge of the sump to the level of the edging bricks and hold it in position with short lengths of duct tape.

8 Screeding the concrete
Use the jigsaw to cut the profile board to shape. Make sure the profile allows for an adequate thickness of concrete as illustrated in the diagram on page 84. Trowel a thick, dry concrete mix inside the pond and use the board to assist in spreading it smoothly.

9 Applying the mosaic
Cut out a fish shape from the card and use this to mark out the design. Break the tiles into small pieces and stick them down. When completed, wipe grout into the gaps and allow to dry. Position the pump in the sump and cover with cobbles.

Split-level pool

If you have a sloping or terraced area in your garden it is a good idea to take advantage of the changes in level and build a stream (see page 42) or split-level pools like these. Plan the project so you can see and hear the waterfall while sitting in your favorite spot. The spray from the waterfall will stain the surrounding brickwork and algae will grow on the brick. Over years this will look more and more attractive.

Considering the design

Remember that the water will splash outwards as far as it has fallen, so do not make the bottom pond too small or you will have damp and slippery areas outside the pond as well as lose considerable amounts of water. When you have a waterfall you also get a fair amount of evaporation so you will want to consider an automatic top-up system.

Getting started

There will be a good deal of excavated soil generated in the excavation of this project, so make sure you have planned where it is to go before you start work.

Overall dimensions and general notes

This split-level design takes a lot of planning but is certainly worth achieving. It is a great way of combining fish, still-water plants and a classic waterfall feature.

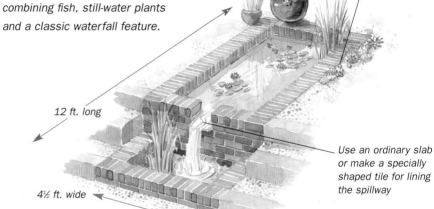

Plan the construction so that both ponds finish at ground level

12 ft. long

4½ ft. wide

Use an ordinary slab or make a specially shaped tile for lining the spillway

You will need

Materials

- ✔ Gravel: 17½ cu. ft.
- ✔ Concrete: 1 part cement (1,650 lb.) and 4 parts ballast (6,600 lb.)
- ✔ Blocks: 35
- ✔ Bricks: 134 (edging) and 432 (brick spacing and walls)
- ✔ Tile: 1⅛ in. x 8 in. x 9¾ in. (for spillway), can be a flat tile or a specially made ceramic or concrete shape
- ✔ Mortar: 1 part cement (330 lb.) and 3 parts sand (990 lb.)

- ✔ Geotextile: 39 sq. yd.
- ✔ Glue: quick drying (for sticking geotextile to wall)
- ✔ Duct tape
- ✔ EPDM: 1 piece 8½ ft. x 13 ft. and 1 piece 7½ ft. x 8½ ft.
- ✔ Plastic pipe: 1 piece 13 ft. long (delivery pipe) and 1 piece to protect electric cable (length to suit your site)
- ✔ Tanking paint: 19 sq. yd. coverage
- ✔ Pump

Tools

- ✔ Tape measure, pegs, string and a piece of chalk
- ✔ Spade, fork and shovel
- ✔ Spirit level
- ✔ Line set
- ✔ Brick hammer
- ✔ Bricklayer's trowel and pointing trowel
- ✔ Scissors
- ✔ Hacksaw
- ✔ Float
- ✔ Paint brush

Cross-section of the split-level pool

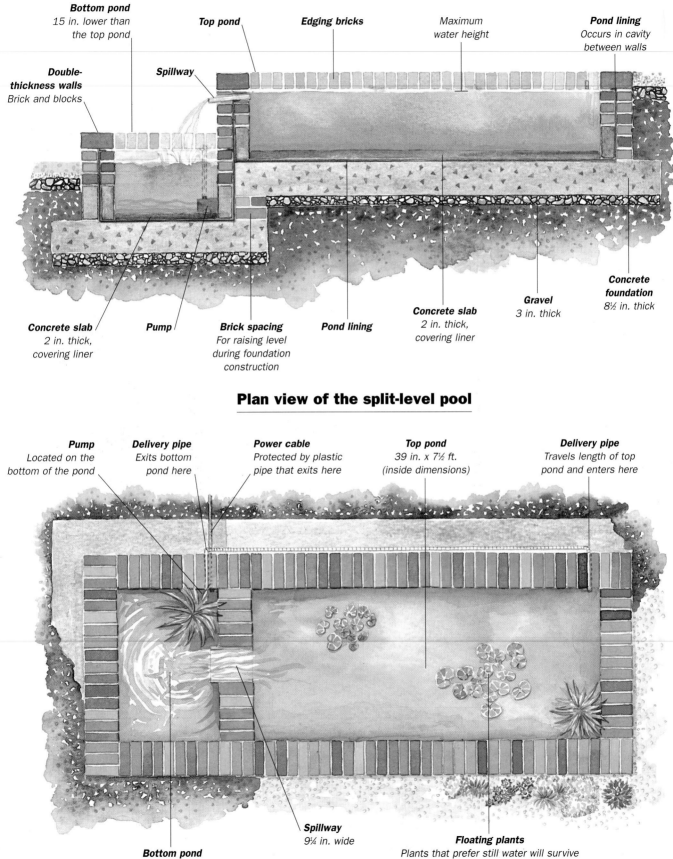

Bottom pond
15 in. lower than the top pond

Top pond

Edging bricks

Maximum water height

Pond lining
Occurs in cavity between walls

Double-thickness walls
Brick and blocks

Spillway

Concrete slab
2 in. thick, covering liner

Pump

Brick spacing
For raising level during foundation construction

Pond lining

Concrete slab
2 in. thick, covering liner

Gravel
3 in. thick

Concrete foundation
8½ in. thick

Plan view of the split-level pool

Pump
Located on the bottom of the pond

Delivery pipe
Exits bottom pond here

Power cable
Protected by plastic pipe that exits here

Top pond
39 in. x 7½ ft. (inside dimensions)

Delivery pipe
Travels length of top pond and enters here

Spillway
9¼ in. wide

Bottom pond
39 in. x 27 in. (inside dimensions)

Floating plants
Plants that prefer still water will survive in the top pond (not the bottom pond)

Exploded view of the split-level pool (lining not shown)

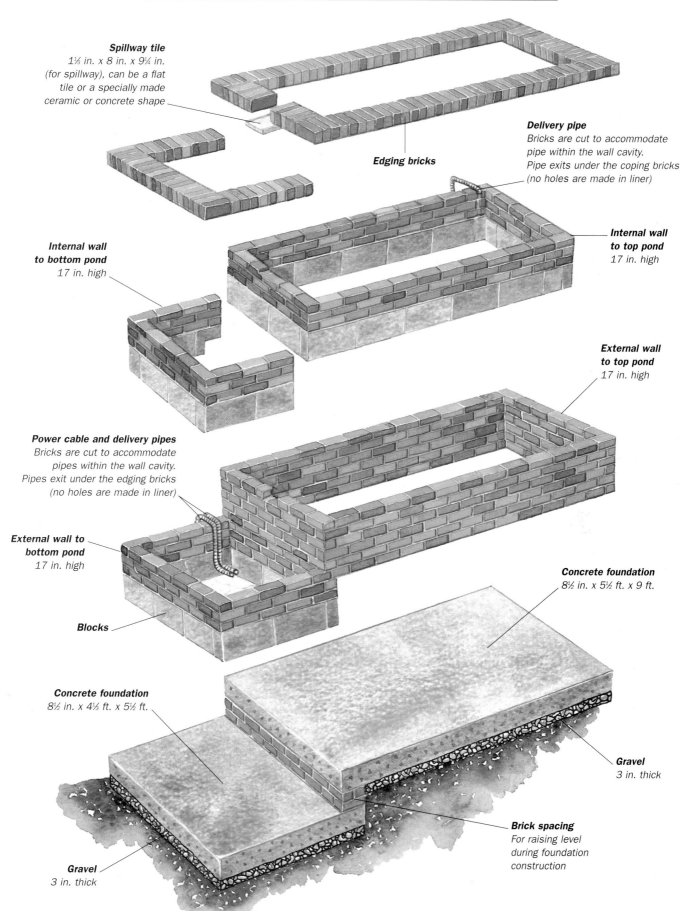

Spillway tile
1⅛ in. x 8 in. x 9¼ in.
(for spillway), can be a flat
tile or a specially made
ceramic or concrete shape

Delivery pipe
Bricks are cut to accommodate
pipe within the wall cavity.
Pipe exits under the coping bricks
(no holes are made in liner)

Edging bricks

**Internal wall
to bottom pond**
17 in. high

**Internal wall
to top pond**
17 in. high

**External wall
to top pond**
17 in. high

Power cable and delivery pipes
Bricks are cut to accommodate
pipes within the wall cavity.
Pipes exit under the edging bricks
(no holes are made in liner)

**External wall to
bottom pond**
17 in. high

Blocks

Concrete foundation
8½ in. x 5½ ft. x 9 ft.

Concrete foundation
8½ in. x 4⅓ ft. x 5½ ft.

Gravel
3 in. thick

Brick spacing
For raising level
during foundation
construction

Gravel
3 in. thick

91

Making the split-level pool

1 Excavating
Mark out the area of the foundation slabs for both ponds. Dig down to a depth of 34 in. Spread hardcore in the bottoms of the holes, compact it to a thickness of 3 in. with a sledgehammer and cast the $8\frac{1}{2}$ in. thick concrete slabs.

2 Building the exterior walls
Mark out the size and positions of the exterior walls. Build up the exterior walls to a height of 17 in. using blocks for the first course and bricks for the rest. Clean up all the joints between the bricks that will remain visible.

3 Lining with geotextile
Remove or flatten any sharp objects and carefully line the entire area with geotextile right to the top, folding or cutting away darts formed at the corners, and sticking it to the walls with quick-drying glue. Trim off any geotextile that rises above the top of the walls.

4 Lining with EPDM
Position the EPDM liner over the geotextile, and use bricks wrapped in geotextile to push the liner into the corners. If necessary refold the creases to make them even and use tape to hold the EPDM in place. Trim the liner 4 in. above the top of the bricks.

5 Fitting the pipework
Install a pipe to carry water from the pump in the bottom pond to the far end of the top pond. The second pipe is for the power cable. The pipes do not pierce the liner; they travel up the wall (in the cavity) and over the top (under the coping).

6 Laying more geotextile

Remove the wrapped bricks and reline the hole with a second layer of geotextile as before taking great care not to damage or pierce the EPDM. Hang the liner over the top of the EPDM at the top of the brickwork.

7 Building the interior walls

Use more blocks and bricks to build interior walls allowing a $\frac{1}{3}$ in. cavity and making a combined wall thickness of $8\frac{1}{2}$ in. Finish at the same height as the exterior wall. You will need to cut blocks and bricks to accommodate the plastic pipes.

8 Fitting the edging bricks

Trim the geotextile level with the top of the walls and trim the EPDM again leaving just 2 in. for folding over. Lay the edging bricks around the edge on a bed of mortar. You will need to cut a few bricks to accommodate the plastic pipes.

9 Laying the concrete bottom

Lay a 2 in. thick concrete slab over the liner in the bottom of the pond. After it has set paint the interior of the pond with black tanking paint and allow to dry completely. Fit the tile in the spillway and install the pump. Let everything dry before filling with water.

Acknowledgments

The vision and skill of Rosemary Wilkinson made this book possible. Clare Sayer ably realised and edited the work and, with the help of the Bridgewaters, has produced a work of which we can all be proud .

I found the space between concept and reality something of a curate's egg and could not have persisted without Clare's charming prompts, Jane, David and the support and help of many who shall remain nameless.

Anthony Archer-Wills first inspired me as to the mysteries of water whilst I was at Merrist Wood College, tutored by Paul Colinridge, Tony Begg, Pauline May and Geoff Ace. The demands of workmates, students and clients with the knowledge and pain gained working with Anthony made necessary this primer about ponds.

My gratitude to the above as well as, to name a few: Mr and Mrs A D Allanson, Mr and Mrs J Ashpool, Mr and Mrs D Bradbury, Mrs P Brenan, Mr and Mrs P Corbett, Ms X Coventry, Mr and Mrs H Davies, P G Jeeves, Mr and Mrs I Keith, Mr David Kiff and Berkeley Homes, Mr and Mrs P Graves, Harveys, Hirsts, Lulubelle for inspiration, Mr and Mrs W Matthews, Mr and Mrs G David Neame, Mr and Mrs W Nicholson, Ms Poppy Totman, Robbie and Rosina, Mr and Mrs J Simon, Sonya, Toby Wear, Véronique and the pond makers of England.

I would also like to thank the following people for letting us photograph their ponds: Linda Davis (page 7), Major L Cave (pages 14 and 32), Mrs J Isaacs (page 43), Gillian Harris (page 47), Anne-Marie Bulat/John Brookes (pages 59 and 89), Camilla Hyde (page 65) and Mr and Mrs Shepard Walwyn (page 77).

New Holland Publishers (UK) Ltd would like to thank the following companies for supplying pictures: Forsham Cottage Arks, (page 15) and OASE (page 19 bottom right: lights). See Suppliers on page 95 for further details.

Index

DATE DUE

AUG 2 1 2006		
AUG 0 6 2007		
FEB 2 1 2008		
AUG 0 6 2012		
JUN 3 0 2013		

DEMCO 138298